Economics for a Fairer Society

Tim Gooding

Economics for a Fairer Society

Going Back to Basics using Agent-Based Models

palgrave
macmillan

Tim Gooding
Kingston University
Kingston upon Thames, UK

ISBN 978-3-030-17019-6   ISBN 978-3-030-17020-2   (eBook)
https://doi.org/10.1007/978-3-030-17020-2

Cover illustration: © Harvey Loake

This Palgrave Pivot imprint is published by the registered company Springer Nature Switzerland AG
The registered company address is: Gewerbestrasse 11, 6330 Cham, Switzerland

CONTENTS

LIST OF FIGURES

LIST OF TABLES

CHAPTER 1

Introduction

Abstract This book invites you to explore the foundational forces of trade in a complex system. While complexity science transformed the physical sciences in the 1970s, economics has held fast to its 100-year tradition of using linear-system mathematical models to build the theory presented in undergraduate university courses around the world. As a result, trade in a complex system is under-researched. Furthermore, there is increasing pressure on the economics discipline to broaden its accepted theory, especially as it is taught in university. This book is about expanding our understanding of economic processes by exploring the outcomes of trade in a complex system when all complications are removed. If the economy is a complex system, then this work presents initial experiments revealing the basic theory of trade.

Keywords Basic economics · Complexity · Trade · Agent-based models · Netlogo · Change · Kuhn

Economists wield one of the most influential theories in modern society. If we get it right, the economy can be tuned to reward people in a fair manner, offering a firm foundation on which we can build a pleasant and prosperous society. If we get it wrong, economic rewards will become detached from effort and service. In this case, undeserving people will be able to bask in the sunshine of wealth while hard-working people can be condemned to the cold shadows of poverty. Over time, such outcomes

T. Gooding, *Economics for a Fairer Society*,
https://doi.org/10.1007/978-3-030-17020-2_1

can lead to rot in the foundations of society creating a dangerous situation for rich and poor alike. Economic theory matters.

This book invites you on a journey to explore one of the most unexplored regions of economics: trade in a complex system. The assumption underlying all this work is that the economy is a complex system. The emphasis of this book is on building and expanding our understandings, not criticising the very large body of linear-system theory that underpins academic economics today.

A great deal has been learned from linear-system analyses, the primary tool used by economists for over a century. The century-long use of equation-based research has shaped the nature of economic research questions and canon. What is possible to explore using mathematical equations has largely been explored. What is not has largely been ignored. For example, there are no linear-system models exploring the macro outcome of changing the distance that agents detect sellers and buyers in a system. This is not because economists are unintelligent, but because equation-based models do not lend themselves to this kind of analysis.

If your tool is a hammer, what you look for are nails. The more intelligent you are, the better you are at finding nails. There is nothing intrinsically wrong with nails or hammers. However, if all you have known before is the linear-system economic theory taught to undergraduate university students, it is possible that you will be shocked by the behaviour of trade in a complex system.

In order to examine complex systems, a relevant tool must be used. This work uses agent-based models (computational economics) because it is one of the few tools that can directly investigate emergent behaviour and evolution in trading environments. All the models shown here are built in Netlogo (Wilensky, 1999), an academic multi-agent programming language designed to help teach multi-agent programming to university students. The models used in this book can be downloaded and run on most home computers. You can test the experimental conclusions for yourself or run experiments for your own purposes.

Some readers experienced with multi-agent models might wonder: why use Netlogo? Isn't Netlogo for amateurs who have yet to learn how to program in a *proper* language? There are several reasons why Netlogo is a sound modelling choice for this work.

First, much of this work seeks to understand the core properties of trade. This is where things are the simplest and, accordingly, much of the experimentation presented in this book uses a simple model. We do not require such things as supercomputers, C++ or Phython, or multiple threading. On the other hand, the last Netlogo model used in this work includes 'living' agents—populations of mortal agents that give birth and nurture children, have evolving propensities, can starve to death, etc. Starvation indicates a failure of distribution, a core economic competency. It is not possible to explore the economics of starvation, for example, in models where life is assumed. If we are already exploring economics beyond most existing models, why do we need a tool even more capable? Finally, Netlogo is one of the most accessible agent-based model languages in existence, with a large online support base. On the whole, Netlogo ticks a lot of boxes.

This book is about economy theory and will not teach you how to program agent-based models. If you are looking for an instructional book on agent-based modelling in economics, there are already good books on the market (e.g. Hamill & Gilbert, 2016; Miller & Page, 2009; Railsback & Grimm, 2011; Wilensky & Rand, 2015).

This book is about moving forward. Where possible, it avoids repeating past criticisms of linear-system economics. There already exists a comprehensive literature challenging the validity of the economic theory as it is taught in universities. In fact, at the time of writing, there is a potential revolution brewing in economics.

Economics is a discipline dogged by criticism from within and without. University students have organised themselves to demand that the undergraduate curriculum be changed (Rethinking Economics) and have recently published what they hope will become a new pluralistic textbook (Fischer et al., 2017). The UK's main academic economic research funding source, the Economic and Social Research Council (ESRC), has funded multi-million-pound programmes called 'Rebuilding Macroeconomics' and 'Rebuilding Microeconomics'. There are established critical books such as *Doughnut Economics* (Raworth, 2017), *Debunking Economics* (Keen, 2011), and *The Origin of Wealth* (Beinhocker, 2006). A top mainstream economist, Paul Romer, recently published a scathing indictment of his profession called '*The Problem with Macroeconomics*' (Romer, 2016). The Institute of New Economic Thinking (INET) has an article on their website called *Publishing and Promotion in Economics: The Tyranny of the Top Five* (Skidelsky et al., n.d.), exploring how and why the top five ranked economic journals promote only a narrow band of research while economists publishing in the top five have the best chances of being hired, getting funding, and being promoted. As early as 1977, physicists have been so fed up with economic theory taught in university that they started building their own theory, possibly starting with Osborne (1977). As a group, they are now called econophysicists. In 1983, a mathematician described 'How Economists Misuse Mathematics' (Blatt, 1983). Meanwhile, in the real world where economic theory influences millions of lives, policy largely based on linear system economic models led the population first to an asset bleeding financial crash, and then to 'austerity', a policy that has led to people to die in the UK from lack of money (Watkins et al., 2017). Some millionaires, such as Nick Hanauer, see today's high wealth inequality as a direct result of the implementation of linear-system economic policies.

This is not an exhaustive list of the disquiet surrounding the economics profession. However, the general atmosphere needs to be noted as the environment in which this book was written.

As Kuhn (2012) pointed out, new knowledge can trigger a crisis in scientific disciplines, especially where it touches on core beliefs. For example, at the beginning of the twentieth century, quantum mechanics shocked classical physics with traits that were completely unintuitive and challenged their beliefs about how the universe worked. Many classical physicists resisted, perhaps the most notable being Max Planck himself who, after making one of the key breakthroughs of quantum physics (the quantum), spent years trying to explain his own discovery in a less revolutionary way (McEvoy & Zarate, 2014, p. 43). Eventually all physicists accepted quantum physics and all its implications. As a result, today, I can type on a computer built using knowledge developed from quantum physics.

This crisis of new knowledge was repeated half way through the twentieth century when complexity reared its unwelcome head. In the 1950s, both Alan Turing and Boris Belousov had made significant complexity discoveries. While Turing's work was cut short when he was arrested for being a homosexual and subsequently died, Belousov's repeatable experiment was dismissed as impossible. Belousov was so disheartened that he walked away from science altogether.

What was being challenged was a deeply embedded Newtonian philosophy built on linear-system theory and models. Many established scientists resisted accepting the new knowledge as it challenged their core beliefs about how the entire universe worked. Eventually, the evidence became so overwhelming that those continuing to resist risked becoming irrelevant.

Complexity was finally accepted into the bosom of science some years after Edward Lorenz's (1963) now famous paper concerning the 'Butterfly Effect'. Today, Belousov's disgraced complexity experiment forms the basis of an entire section of chemical study called the BZ reaction, while Turing is acknowledged as one of the first mathematicians to grasp the relevance of emergent behaviour in biology.

It has been over half a century since complexity revolutionised the thinking in the physical sciences. In 2019, the economics discipline still trains students to think in terms of linear-system dynamics as explained by equation-based models. This creates a built-in resistance to complexity that has become woven throughout society. Just as was the case in physics, accepting complexity into mainstream economic theory will involve changing some core beliefs that almost everyone has about the free market.

Kuhn noted how science moves through long periods of consolidation punctuated with scientific leaps. This book invites you to leap into the basic behaviour of trade in a complex environment.

Chapter 3 briefly describes complexity and some of its terms as it applies to this work. Chapters 4–7 describe the history of agent-based modelling and introduces some key ideas necessary to understand the experimental section. Chapters 8–15 describe the experiments in as it affects equality, price, and the 'life' of a living population. Also explored is the outcome of two different economic systems being overlaid onto a 'living' population. The final experimental chapter compares the economic predictions in an identical model populated by 'eternal' agents and populated with 'mortal' agents.

But first, the empirical experience and observations underpinning this research are described in Chapter 2. This work was not born in a classroom or office, but in the fierce beauty of the Yukon Territories.

References

Beinhocker, E. D. (2006). *The origin of wealth: Evolution—Complexity, and the radical remaking of economics.* Cambridge, MA: Harvard Business School Press.

Blatt, J. (1983). How economists misuse mathematics. In *Why economics is not yet a science* (pp. 166–186). London: Palgrave Macmillan.

Fischer, L., Hasell, J., Proctor, J. C., Uwakwe, D., Perkins, Z. W., & Watson, C. (Eds.). (2017). *Rethinking economics: An introduction to pluralist economics*. London: Routledge.

Hamill, L., & Gilbert, N. (2016). *Agent-based modelling in economics*. Chichester: Wiley.

Keen, S. (2011). *Debunking economics: The naked emperor dethroned?*. London: Zed Books.

Kuhn, T. S. (2012). *The structure of scientific revolutions*. Chicago: University of Chicago Press.

Lorenz, E. N. (1963). Deterministic nonperiodic flow. *Journal of the Atmospheric Sciences, 20*(2), 130–141.

McEvoy, J. P., & Zarate, O. (2014). *Introducing quantum theory: A graphic guide*. London: Icon Books.

Miller, J. H., & Page, S. E. (2009). *Complex adaptive systems: An introduction to computational models of social life* (Vol. 17). Princeton: Princeton University Press.

Osborne, M. F. (1977). *Stock market and finance from a physicist's viewpoint*. Minneapolis: Crossgar Press.

Railsback, S. F., & Grimm, V. (2011). *Agent-based and individual-based modeling: A practical introduction*. Princeton: Princeton University Press.

Raworth, K. (2017). *Doughnut economics: Seven ways to think like a 21st-century economist*. Chelsea Green Publishing.

Romer, P. (2016). The trouble with macroeconomics. *The American Economist, 20*, 1–20.

Skidelsky, R., Heckman, J., Moktan, S., Schröder, E., Storm, S., Semieniuk, G., ... Basu, K. (n.d.). *Publishing and promotion in economics: The tyranny of the top five*. Retrieved from https://www.ineteconomics.org/research/research-papers/publishing-and-promotion-in-economics-the-tyranny-of-the-top-five.

Watkins, J., Wulaningsih, W., Da Zhou, C., Marshall, D. C., Sylianteng, G. D., Rosa, P. G. D., ... Maruthappu, M. (2017). Effects of health and social care spending constraints on mortality in England: A time trend analysis. *BMJ Open, 7*(11), e017722.

Wilensky, U. (1999). *Netlogo*. Evanston, IL: Center for Connected Learning and Computer-Based Modeling, Northwestern University. http://ccl.northwestern.edu/Netlogo/.

Wilensky, U., & Rand, W. (2015). *An introduction to agent-based modeling: Modeling natural, social, and engineered complex systems with Netlogo*. Cambridge: MIT Press.

CHAPTER 2

First Nation Transition

Abstract Useful theories have roots deep in reality. This work was inspired through witnessing the impact of transforming a First Nations community into a capitalistic community. As intended, the community, in aggregate, got richer. However, community rifts intensified, with some people feeling as if they had been bypassed altogether. In fact, many of the endemic 'modern' problems found fertile ground in the newly capitalistic community. In searching for practical answers to what I was witnessing, a key research question came into being: in practical terms, what is the root cause of persistent problems plaguing modern societies?

Keywords First nation · Economic transition · Inequality · Modern problems · Emergent behaviour · Evolutionary prerequisites · Research question

The inspiration for this work began in the mountains and rivers of the Yukon Territories in Canada. In 1991, I was hired by the Little/Salmon Carmacks First Nation to be their Economic Development Officer. My task was to facilitate the transition of their community to a self-supporting free-market society within five years.

Carmacks was a remote northern community populated by a few hundred people mainly living in a piece of land embraced by the Yukon river. Though most did not, I lived in a log cabin with no running water or

T. Gooding, *Economics for a Fairer Society*,
https://doi.org/10.1007/978-3-030-17020-2_2

electricity. I used a wood stove for heat, paraffin and oil lamps for light, and an outhouse. I never experienced temperatures below −57 °C. If anyone wants to know a trick for enjoying a warm comfortable outdoor toilet seat in −50 °C temperatures while using no power of any sort, I'm your economist.

The community was in distress. At the beginning of the twentieth century, residence schools were introduced to modernise the First Nation people. The idea was to remove young children from their home and place them in distant residence schools where immersive education would replace native traditions and language with European speech, values, and goals. The physical, sexual, and mental abuse that took place in these residence schools was widespread and is well documented.

One of the effects was the creation of a rift between the generations. Parents and elders had little experience with abused children, and it was increasingly difficult for them to create meaningful intergenerational connections. As their society's vast store of knowledge resided in intergenerational stories, poor communication between the generations crippled their society's potential. Alcoholism became increasingly common and the community became increasingly dependent on government handouts to survive.

Change accelerated when the Alaska Highway was built in 1941. Old-world immigrants found the new road quite convenient. Private property became more common and hunting stocks were reduced. Overall, the effectiveness of traditional techniques was being weakened, furthering the argument that traditional indigenous communities were poor models to follow in the modern age.

Despite this, when I first entered the community, there was hope. Throughout the disruption, their community had retained enough tradition that many still felt their community was generally supportive of individuals. With self-governance on the horizon and the promised rewards of free-market participation, people looked forward to the future.

I was hired by the First Nation to implement the free-market transition of their community. My undergraduate economics degree gave me the theory and over a decade of working in various market sectors grounded that theory in reality. While the theory spoke of capitalism as a near utopian possibility (increasing productivity, maximising utility, individual liberty), my experience lent me caution.

With all this in mind, a five-year community development plan, funded by the Canadian government, was put into motion. Using a combination of education, healing, incentive, and experience, the First Nation leadership and myself set to work turning the residents into good free-market citizens capable of holding down modern jobs. We had to tackle some very basic concepts. For example, 'on time' in a hunter/gatherer sense is entirely from '8:30 am sharp'. We rewarded those who best developed free-market habits with good jobs and money. Those who failed to conform to free-market behaviour remained poor. We offered them new and varied conformation training and personal healing whenever funding became available.

A few individuals transitioned out of poverty by becoming good workers who hold down well-paying jobs. Some became very successful. However, in general, this was not an easy task. While traditional life has community obligations, traditional life also encourages individuals to be their own authority in their daily lives. Training someone to lay down their self-empowerment in exchange for spending the day doing another's bidding was not always easy to sell. Furthermore, well-paying jobs were not endless. The divide between the 'haves' and the 'have-nots' increased, stressing the community's established ties.

I cannot report an objective measure from my experience. Subjectively, I experienced a community transition from one that was relatively money poor, tightly knit, generally supportive, to one that was better off by aggregate measures, but increasingly divided. The 'have-nots' were becoming increasingly bitter about their continuing poverty while the 'haves' were developing an increasing sense of frustration in trying to help and motivate the 'have-nots'. If only we could get the failures to make the *right* choices. While there were always one or two individual successes that gave hope, the overall problem remained stubbornly immutable, much like many social problems in modern society.

This was not the only indigenous community that experienced a degrading influence arising from increased financial success. In Hobbema (now called Maskwacis) in Alberta, Canada, a large oil reserve was discovered. As part of the deal to extract the oil, the indigenous community living above the oil were given extraordinary monetary benefits. Before they even got out of bed, a family of four would make enough money to be considered well-off. Matters were designed so that anyone turning 18 years of age would be given enough money to attend any University in the world. Thriving upmarket shops sprung up to surround the community. According to the free-market narrative, the Hobbema community had hit the jackpot of happiness.

Meanwhile, back in reality, their social indicators plummeted. One figure made it into the papers: their youth suicide rates rose to over 83 times that of the Canadian national average for males and 160 times the national average for young women (Stolte, 2011). While the experiences of Hobbema, and other Native American communities, were discussed at length among the First Nations, no long-term solution was found. Wherever the world's resources are controlled by the free market, choosing not to participate results in life-threatening poverty.

It would be simplistic to suggest that the influx of money alone caused these problems. In discussions with other economic development officers, it was apparent that the increased purchase power was accompanied by a loss of traditional supportive networks and general contentment with life. In other words, the inherent structure of the free market was creating circumstances that changed the shape of communities in a manner that was causing social harm. This effect was made obvious by the very rapid transitions that were going on in the Native American communities at that time. Community values were being rapidly shifted to capitalistic ones in Native communities up and down Canada. Before and after was being starkly presented to those involved.

These ground observations have subsequently been supported by academic work. Diener and Diener (1995) found that suicide rates were inversely correlated with GDP. More recently, Oishi and Diener (2014) found that poorer populations had a greater sense of meaning in life than richer populations. Apparently, the wealthier nations get, the more likely it becomes that their citizens will commit suicide and the less likely they will find meaning in life. At the time, I knew none of this. All I had was the Utopian theory of perfect competition and my observations of reality.

The next years were spent seeking a practical cause for what I had witnessed in the hope of finding real solutions. At that time, my only clue was something tenuous and unscientific.

A Yukoner telling another Yukoner they are going 'outside' meant they were going on a trip south of the Yukon. People living in the Yukon (except perhaps Whitehorse) live a life heavily shaped by practicality enforced by nature.

In the 1990s, the Yukon was populated by 30,000 people in an area near to the size of the UK, 20,000 of whom lived in the capital. The lack of human domination over the environment necessitated a real-world pragmatism linked to nature and life. This resulted in an inclusive and supportive culture. When Yukoners travelled south, it seemed to the traveller that they leave pragmatism and enter worlds shaped by strange and artificial desires, habits, and beliefs, all of which were detached from important elements of relationship, community, and survival. Stepping off an aeroplane into a large city like Vancouver or Calgary really did feel like one had arrived on 'Mars'.

In early winter morning in the Yukon, I could go for a walk and feel like the only person on earth. It was dark and cold, so there was little turbulence disturbing with air. Except when the northern lights or the moon lit the landscape, stars hung bright and clear in the sky and satellites could be seen moving past with startlingly clarity. When I stood completely still holding my breath, the only sound I could hear was my heart beat.

During these walks, I would frequently take some time to listen to the world's news and discussions on a portable radio. From my 'outside' viewpoint, the strange goings on in the alien world beyond the Yukon began to, in my mind's eye, take on shapes that looked as if people were being moulded by invisible global forces rather than their own desires and decisions. Five years later, I found the concept of complexity. Specifically, I noticed that the prerequisites for evolutionary problem-solving systems were boldly present in modern society. Coincidentally perhaps, these prerequisites predicted the same shapes that my mind's eye perceived from my vantage point of the Yukon. Eventually, I published a paper describing experiments that captured the evolutionary prerequisites existing in modern global society (Gooding, 2014).

At the heart of all modern economies is trade. Trade in a complex system behaves quite differently from the predictions of linear-system equations, especially when evolutionary prerequisites are present. This work explores the core complexity patterns generated by trade in its simplest form and how these patterns influence such things as wealth distribution, price, and efficiency.

REFERENCES

Diener, E., & Diener, C. (1995). The wealth of nations revisited: Income and quality of life. *Social Indicators Research, 36*(3), 275–286.

Gooding, T. (2014). Modelling society's evolutionary forces. *Journal of Artificial Societies and Social Simulation, 17*(3), 3.

Oishi, S., & Diener, E. (2014). Residents of poor nations have a greater sense of meaning in life than residents of wealthy nations. *Psychological Science, 25*(2), 422–430.

Stolte, E. (2011, December 17). Oil brought money to Hobbema, Alta. Reserve, along with alcohol, drugs, and murder. *Postmedia News,* Canada.

[Note: The source material/statistics for this article is a 1984 study done by the Canadian Federal government that was never released but had been leaked. That leak, which I have seen, has since become unavailable.]

CHAPTER 3

Complexity, Emergence, and Evolution

Abstract Most economists are not familiar with complexity science as it applies to economics. Complexity and emergent behaviour are broad terms that are not scientifically defined. This chapter outlines how the terms complexity, emergent behaviour, and evolution are being used in this work. While mainly aimed at people who are not familiar with complexity, it also explains how these terms are specifically being used in this work. It also defines two new terms that clarify certain aspects of evolution as it applies to economics, specifically, the 'fitness test' and 'evolutionary strength'.

Keywords Complexity · Emergent behaviour · Evolutionary · Fitness test · Evolutionary strength

Most of today's economists do not know how complexity science is relevant to economics.

Veblen (1898) formally suggested making economics an evolutionary science. Soon after, Schumpeter attempted to describe innovative evolutionary processes as a key driver in capitalistic economies (Schumpeter, 1912). However, Schumpeter had no means to experimentally test his hypotheses. As time went by, the increasing availability of computing power allowed Arthur (1989) to model innovation using agent-based models (ABMs) and discovered aspects of innovation that Schumpeter never imagined.

© The Author(s) 2019
T. Gooding, *Economics for a Fairer Society*,
https://doi.org/10.1007/978-3-030-17020-2_3

Regardless, a proper scientific investigation of market evolutionary forces never occurred. To date, evolutionary economics starts with the assumptions that the economy is 'Darwinian' (Witt, 2008). However, this is based on metaphors of nature rather than scientific certainties. This ambiguity may be the reason that, 'there is little agreement among the researchers in the field when it comes to deciding what is specific about evolutionary economics' (Witt, 2008, p. 570).

As we will see, market economy evolution is specific enough to facilitate repeatable scientific experiments. It does not require metaphors or analogies. Evolution can be triggered using established evolutionary prerequisites (see Chapter 6). As these prerequisites exist in trade markets, investigating evolutionary market properties is simply a matter of placing established observable evolutionary prerequisites in models and observing the outcome. As practical evolutionary economics is so new, a few terms need to be defined before we proceed.

Entire books have been devoted to explaining complexity, emergence, and evolution. One of the earliest that is still relevant and accessible is *Chaos: Making a New Science* by Gleick (1988). There is also a great deal of information and videos on the internet.

The brief definitions in this chapter are offered mainly to help those with little or no background in complexity to understand the experiments in this work. However, because evolutionary investigations are so new to economics, economic definitions have not really been developed. Accordingly, some terms have been specifically developed for this work.

3.1   Defining Complexity

Complexity is not scientifically defined (e.g. Edmonds, 1995; Standish, 2001), but instead characterised in various ways depending on how it is to be applied. In economics, perhaps the best way to characterise complexity is by comparing it to linear-system theory.

A linear-system economic analysis depends on established relationships between defined economic variables. Econometrics determine the historical correlations of these variables over time in the hopes of being able to formalise the relationships into mathematical equations. The equations representing individual relationships are then grouped together to form an overall model of the economy. This system of equations is then simultaneously solved. The key assumption that enables mathematical solutions to be found at all is that the resting state of a free-market economy is an equilibrium. Much of 2019 economic theory would vanish were this one assumption removed. In complex system models, an equilibrium need not be assumed.

Another difference is that history matters in complex system models. Current undergraduate economic models go from one equilibrium state to another after one or more variables in the equations are changed. This sequence models two states of the economy. By contrast, in complex system models, every iteration features a new state. If the model is run for 10,000 iterations, there are 10,000 different states, with each previous state influencing the following states.

The third difference is that complex system models need not assume that historical correlations are valid in the future. While understanding current relationships is important work, complex system models allow for adaptation and evolution. These two processes can endogenously change the relationship between variables, sometimes radically. Empirical linear-system models rely on fixed relationships. If there is any change, a linear-system model needs to be redesigned.

Complex system models allow for such things as feedback, agent heterogeneity and adaptation over time, and success imitation. This frequently involves the modelling of many heterogenous agents. By contrast, undergraduate microeconomics is frequently the study of two representative agents interacting, while macroeconomics is the study of one representative agent interacting with the world. In this work, the model used to explore the most basic charactertistics of trade uses 400 agents. These agents can be set to be homogeneous, heterogenous, or evolutionary, depending on what is being investigated.

Overall, complexity is a vast field that includes such things as network theory, emergent behaviour, system dynamics, and evolution. This work concentrates on the results of agent-based model experiments. When these experiments are configured not to evolve, the most interesting results are emergent patterns.

3.2   Defining and Detecting Emergent Behaviour

It is often said that one of the greatest advantages of agent-based modelling is their ability to generate emergent behaviour. However, as Christen and Franklin (2002) ask, 'emergence is everywhere...but what is it'? Their paper explores the lack of scientific consensus concerning the definition of emergence and emergent behaviour.

Christen and Franklin completed what they acknowledge as a flawed survey (because of the low response rate) of the Santa Fe Institute (SFI) and the students attending the SFI's Complex System's Summer School. Of the responders, "15% of students and 33% of researchers think that 'emergence' is a buzzword to be avoided, while 22% of students and 16% of researchers think that it is a filler term which should be replaced when an entity is understood" (Christen & Franklin, 2002, Section 5.4, paragraph 2).

One problem might be the tendency for subjective terms to creep into the definition of 'emergence' and 'emergent behaviour'. Railsback and Grimm (2011, p. 101) suggest, 'The key question about emergence is this: what dynamics of the system and what model outcomes emerge — arise in relatively complex and unpredictable ways — from what behaviours of the agents and what characteristics of their environment?' They stress that unpredictable emergence must be separated from outcomes that are 'imposed—forced to occur in direct and predictable ways'. The use of the subjective term 'unpredictable' allows the presence of emergence to be detected, by definition, according to the abilities of the researchers studying them. A system that seems straightforward to an experienced researcher might be bafflingly complex to someone new to the field.

Subjectivity is not the only problem with the definition of emergence. Dessalles and Phan's (Dessalles & Phan 2006) define emergence in this way: 'Formally, in multi-agent systems, emergence is a central property of dynamic systems based upon interacting autonomous entities (the agents). The knowledge of entities' attributes and rules is not sufficient to predict the behaviour of the whole system'. In addition to the subjectivity of 'predict', this definition defines emergence out of existence in systems where agents do not interact. Wilensky and Rand's (2015, p. 6) definition also implies agent interaction as necessary when they say that emergence is 'the arising of novel or coherent structures, patterns, and properties through the interactions of multiple distributed elements'. While their definition emphasises 'interactions', the model they use to exemplify emergent behaviour features no interaction between the agents or between agents and the model's environment (ibid., pp. 7–9).

In building a definition, one key question is how many agents are required before emergence can be present. Consider stigmergy, a property in a system where different agent behaviours are activated by different shapes or states encountered in the environment that the agents themselves have built (Bonabeau, Dorigo, & Theraulaz, 1999; Grassé, 1959). In economics, the Lucas critique (Lucas, 1976) is a single itera-tion of stigmergy. Stigmergy allows termites, for example, to use simple individual rules to build nests at least as complex and efficient as the best that human architects can achieve. These principles are now being used to help architects design better structures (John, Clements-Croome, & Jeronimidis, 2005). Were a single insect given a long enough lifespan and food supply, it is conceivable that it could, as a population of one, complete a nest by following a series of simple behaviour rules. If we insist on populations greater than one before allowing for emergence then where more than one agent builds a nest using simple local rules is considered emergent, when one agent achieves the same thing using the same rules, it is not emergent, by definition.

While it is possible for scientific consensus to rule out emergence wherever the agent population is less than two, I argue that doing so could lead to the occasional thorny classification problem. On the other hand, if we allow, by definition, emergence to arise from a single agent acting in an environment, then to remain consistent, the definition must exclude assertions such as 'interaction between agents'.

With these concepts in mind, we construct the definition of emer-gence for this work. The most important aspect of emergence is that something 'emerges' beyond that which is obviously described by the behaviour of the individual elements of the system. To state this suc-cinctly, we can borrow from Santamaria-Bonfil, Gershenson, and Fernández (2017, p. 1) by stating an emergent system must 'acquire functional/spatial/temporal structures without a priori specifications.'

This next part of the definition seems to cause difficulty. What exactly must be the constituent parts of an emergent system? Must it be 'agents' or 'autonomous entities' or can it involve something else? For example, stigmergy relies on agents interacting with the environment. The envi-ronment in which the agents operate is not usually considered an agent or an autonomous entity. If we allow the agency of emergence to go beyond 'autonomous agents', then the problem is solved. Furthermore, if we allow the observer to be one of the 'autonomous agents', Wilensky and Rand's (2015, pp. 7–9) model designed to demonstrate emergence now falls within the definition of emergence.

If we put all this together, we have a more inclusive definition of emergence. An emergent system is one acquiring functional/spatial/ temporal structures without a priori instruction or specification, arising from the interactions of the system's constituent elements—elements that sometimes include the observer (with a nod to the physicist Heisenberg).

Unfortunately, this definition does not resolve the problem of detection. If a result is declared to be the consequence of 'emergence' or 'emergent behaviour', then 'emergence' requires a clear method of detection (Dessalles & Phan, 2006). This can be resolved by noting that, in practical terms, the prerequisites for emergent behaviour (and evolution) are well understood. This offers the opportunity to reverse the detection problem: instead of seeking a scientific method to identify emergent behaviour in its final manifestation, it is easier to identify, or detect, the presence of the necessary prerequisites.

In simple terms, emergence is whatever arises from an agent(s) acting according to local rules. Evolution arises whenever heterogeneous agents are empowered and/or disempowered in the system according to a fitness function or fitness test (see Sect. 3.3). To my knowledge, it has never been demonstrated that where the prerequisites exist, emergent behaviour or evolution does not result. Until such time, it is reasonable to declare the presence of emergent behaviour or evolution wherever the prerequisites exist. This method simultaneously allows for detection and provides a second clear definition: emergent behaviour and evolution are that which emerge from their known prerequisites.

3.3   EVOLUTION

The minimum conditions necessary to trigger evolution are agent heterogeneity and success imitation. As differences do exist in groups of people and between business, the agents of society are empirically heterogeneous. Success imitation can take many forms such as reading a book about the habits of the rich and powerful or going to university. Regardless of method, we know many people who seek to understand successful traits (How *did* she get that grant?). Empirically, the prerequisites to evolution exist in society. Therefore, evolution.

In the markets, it is even simpler. People, businesses, institutions, and governments are heterogeneous. People, businesses, institutions, and governments all seek to be monetarily successful. Furthermore, many seek to emulate those who have demonstrated success. Hence, evolution—but to what end?

3.3.1 Evolutionary Fitness

In artificial evolutionary systems, the fitness function turns all the aspects of evolutionary fitness an agent can possess and ranks the agent using a single quantitative result. In evolutionary systems, agents performing relatively well according to evolutionary fitness are empowered while those performing poorly are disempowered. This process is predictable enough for engineers to use it to design specific technology. For example, NASA used just such an evolutionary system to develop an aerial successfully used in space on NASA's Space Technology 5 mission (Hornby, Globus, Linden, & Lohn, 2006).

Fitness functions are featured in numerous scientific experiments. They determine the optimisation goal that the agents and, sometimes, the system as a whole will seek to maximise. For example, Hillis (1999) used a number fitness function to evolve agents to sort random sets of numbers in the fewest steps possible. The better the agents sorted numbers, the higher their score. Any agent that achieved a less than average score was eliminated from the population. Those remaining created a new generation of agents using computer code shared by the remaining agents (like biological parents share genes to make a new child). His system was initiated using agents made up of random computer code. What emerged from the evolutionary process were agents that were so efficient at sorting numbers that they challenged the best human-designed programs (Johnson, 2001).

A fitness function can be made up of as many characteristics as the model builder desires. The NASA space aerial had weight and size constraints, as well as performance, energy usage, etc. The final fitness ranking comes from the overall score from all these different characteristics.

Sometimes, the fitness function is not explicit—it simply emerges from the rules of the system. For example, Zykov, Mytilinaios, Adams, and Lipson (2005) demonstrated that in the absence of an explicit fitness function, their evolutionary system defaulted to self-replication. In other words, from the initial chaos, reproducing agents began to appear. This can be anticipated because agents that manage to self-replicate will remain present over time, whereas agents that do not disappear. Over time, the system is increasingly populated by self-replicating agents.

These emerged fitness functions are typical of what is seen in markets and society. However, it would be difficult and possibly highly controversial to specifically suggest that an empirical social fitness function can be recreated. How would we agree on the precise bundle of habits and traits that make a person or business the most successful in the market? Fortunately, there is a much simpler way to reproduce the effectiveness of empirical fitness functions.

3.3.2   Fitness Test

Instead of trying to reproduce an empirical fitness function, it is much easier to identify how the fitness function ranks the agents' performance. For example, society is structured so that there is a very high correlation to money (or wealth) with power. While all the different fitness considerations that contribute to income and wealth are likely impossible to delineate (and were you to succeed in delineating them, you would be wealthy beyond your wildest dreams), it is easy to describe the result of the fitness function. Therefore, we do not attempt to recreate the fitness function. Instead, we identify the fitness function output and allow the system to determine or evolve the fitness function itself. For example, a free market's fitness function could be said to use money and/or wealth as a measure of success. People who are most successful with money are often emulated while those who fail are not. Furthermore, money is highly correlated with real power.

This is not to suggest that there are no other fitness functions present. For career economists, publishing in the top five journals has become part of an evolutionary fitness function. However, even this is ultimately powered by money because publishing in the top five means a greater chance for better paying jobs and research grants.

The term we use to describe the result of the fitness function is *fitness test*. The fitness test is the quantitative result of the dominant fitness function that is used to rank the agents in the system.

Fitness test is used as an abbreviate to the phrase 'measure of evolutionary fitness'. For example, instead of saying, 'the **measure of evolutionary fitness** changed from money to assets', the text will read 'the **fitness test** changed from money to assets'. In a model, a 'money' fitness test means that the agents will be ranked according to their possession of money. Those at the top are the subject of imitation by those with less money. Functionally, changing a fitness test changes the agent rankings. As you will see, this results in the emergence of entirely new patterns.

3.3.3   Evolutionary Solutions

An evolutionary solution is the performance developed by the agent or the system through the processes of evolution to overcome problems in regard to the fitness test or, in engineering in particular, the final solution an evolutionary system was designed achieve. A key property of evolutionary systems is their ability to develop high performing solutions that defy explanation or understanding. For example, Hillis notes:

> One the interesting things about the sorting programs that evolved in my experiment is that I do not understand how they work. I have carefully examined their instruction sequences, but I do not understand them: I have no simpler explanation of how the programs work than the instruction sequences themselves. It may be that the programs are not understandable – that there is no way to break the operation of the program into a hierarchy of understandable parts. (Hillis 1999, pp. 146–147)

However, this must be balanced by Lipson's (2005, p. 151) observation that, 'evolutionary algorithms do not provide guarantees on solution optimality, and do not always find the optimal solution'. In other words, no one quite knows what will emerge from a single evolutionary run. However, as we will see, repeating the evolutionary process increases the chance of strong solutions emerging.

3.4   SUMMARY NOTE

Some of this terminology has been adapted to make it specifically useful in studies of markets and society and is not canon for complexity or evolution. Part of the reason is that, as far as I understand, no one is exploring the impact of the evolutionary prerequisites present in market systems. These terms make this research more succinct. This terminology also emphasises aspects unique to real-world targeted evolutionary systems, as artificial systems generally do not use fitness functions emerging from circumstance.

REFERENCES

Arthur, W. B. (1989). Competing technologies, increasing returns, and lock-in by historical events. *The Economic Journal, 99*(394), 116–131.

Bonabeau, E., Dorigo, M., & Theraulaz, G. (1999). *Swarm intelligence: From natural to artificial systems* (No. 1). New York: Oxford University Press.

Chaos, J. G. (1988). *Making a new science*. Minerva: Minerva.

Christen, M., & Franklin, L. R. (2002). The concept of emergence in complexity science: Finding coherence between theory and practice. In *Proceedings of the Complex Systems Summer School* (Vol. 4).

Dessalles, J. L., & Phan, D. (2006). Emergence in multi-agent systems: Cognitive hierarchy, detection, and complexity reduction part I: Methodological issues. In *Artificial Economics* (pp. 147–159). Springer, Berlin: Heidelberg.

Edmonds, B. (1995). What is complexity? The philosophy of complexity per se with application to some examples in evolution. In *The evolution of complexity*. Dordrecht: Kluwer Academic.

Grassé, P. P. (1959). La reconstruction du nid et les coordinations interindividuelles chezBellicositermes natalensis etCubitermes sp. la théorie de la stigmergie: Essai d'interprétation du comportement des termites constructeurs. *Insectes sociaux, 6*(1), 41–80.

Hillis, W. D. (1999). *The pattern on the stone: The simple ideas that make computers work*. New York: Basic Books (AZ).

Hornby, G., Globus, A., Linden, D., & Lohn, J. (2006). Automated antenna design with evolutionary algorithms. In *Space 2006* (p. 7242).

John, G., Clements-Croome, D., & Jeronimidis, G. (2005). Sustainable building solutions: A review of lessons from the natural world. *Building and Environment, 40*(3), 319–328.

Johnson, S. (2001). *Emergence: The connected lives of ants, brains, cities, and software*. New York: Simon and Schuster.

Lipson, H. (2005). Evolutionary robotics and open-ended design automation. *Biomimetics, 17*(9), 129–155.

Lucas, R. E. (1976, January). Econometric policy evaluation: A critique. In *Carnegie-Rochester Conference Series on Public Policy* (Vol. 1, pp. 19–46), North-Holland.

Railsback, S. F., & Grimm, V. (2011). *Agent-based and individual-based modeling: A practical introduction*. Princeton: Princeton University Press.

Santamaria-Bonfil, G., Gershenson, C., & Fernández, N. (2017). A package for measuring emergence, self-organization, and complexity based on Shannon entropy. *Frontiers in Robotics and AI, 4,* 10.

Schumpeter, J. A. (1912). *Theorie der wirtschaftlichen Entwicklung* (1st ed.) [English translation 1934: *Theory of economic development*. Cambridge, MA: Harvard University Press]. Leipzig: Duncker & Humblot.

Standish, R. K. (2001). On complexity and emergence. *arXiv preprint nlin/ 0101006.*

Veblen, T. (1898). Why is economics not an evolutionary science? *The Quarterly Journal of Economics, 12*(4), 373–397.

Wilensky, U., & Rand, W. (2015). *An introduction to agent-based modeling: Modeling natural, social, and engineered complex systems with Netlogo.* Cambridge: MIT Press.

Witt, U. (2008). What is specific about evolutionary economics? *Journal of Evolutionary Economics, 18*(5), 547–575.

Zykov, V., Mytilinaios, E., Adams, B., & Lipson, H. (2005). Robotics: Self-reproducing machines. *Nature, 435*(7039), 163.

CHAPTER 4

Agent-Based Model History and Development

Abstract Agent-based modelling has a deep rich history. When it began in physics in the 1930s, it immediately resulted in key scientific breakthroughs. Through time, many disciplines both in and outside academia have adopted agent-based modelling for scientific investigation, especially where systems made up of people were concerned. All this makes it an ideal tool with which to investigate the economy.

Keywords Agent-based model history · Agent-based models · FERMIAC · Sugarscape · Microsimulation · Emergent behaviour · Agent-based modelling pitfalls

In the 1980s, and after decades of intensive investigation, biologists still had no idea how birds achieved the coordination required for flocking. One day, a computer scientist was watching birds flock and the answer suddenly came to him. The birds were not coordinated by a leader or by communication of any sort, they were self-organising. In other words, the individual birds were all obeying the same local rules that led to the mesmerising flocking patterns we see in nature. Reynold's (1987) successfully tested his hypothesis by building an agent-based model (ABM).

Seen on a screen, his model looked like a group objects (triangles in one of his simulations, animated birds in another) flocking in a simulated environment. Each object represented a single bird that he called a boid. His model assumed flight and then used three simple rules of behaviour

© The Author(s) 2019
T. Gooding, *Economics for a Fairer Society*,
https://doi.org/10.1007/978-3-030-17020-2_4

that all his boids individually followed: (1) avoid collisions with nearby flockmates; (2) attempt to match velocity with nearby flockmates; (3) attempt to stay close to nearby flockmates. The result was majestic flocking behaviour that we see in the real world.

Today, ABMs are used in many research disciplines to uncover the emergent result of individuals interacting according to individual rules of behaviour. In economics, using agent-based modelling is frequently called computational economics.

Economic ABMs tend program their agents as people, businesses, or institutions. Individual agents might be able to move around their environment, as people do, or remain in one place, such as brick and mortar shops do. One of the key aspects of an ABM is that space and time can be modelled. One person might be right next to another, while a third might be situated some distance away. As we will see, this creates real consequences in the resulting emergent patterns in price, especially where distance effects the likelihood of trade.

Properties of agent-based modelling create unique modelling challenges that do not exist in equation-based models. For example, if the money supply is increased, which agent or agents get the money? It is not realistic to give all agents an equal share—I have never received a share of the annual money supply increase. On the other hand, what rules determine which agents receive the increased purchase power of newly created money whenever M0 or M1 increase?

The other part of an ABM is its environment. In the models in this work, the simulated ground will be made up of a number of patches that can be individually programmed. For example, each patch can have its own fertility or a resistance to harvesting that must be overcome by labour. It is relatively straightforward to create an economic model with real-world environmental constraints and test for system sustainability using ABMs. Equally, we can explore the nature of starvation and how the world has generated a starvation rate that equates to millions of people at the same time it generates a surplus of food.

4.1   History

The ABMs began life in 1933 when the Nobel laureate physicist Enrico Fermi started using mechanical adding machines, or whatever came to hand, as discrete probability generators to make up a model. The result was able to find solutions to previously unyielding physics problems.

With this new technique, he entertained himself by astonishing scientists with far too accurate predictions concerning experimental outcomes (Metropolis, 1987). In physics, this is called the Monte Carlo method and is itself a re-envisioning of statistical sampling, a much older problem-solving method.

Some of the Monte Carlo's most profound results come from extremely simple models. For example, the famous (in physics) FERMIAC machine utilised a pseudo-random number generator to repeatedly calculate three probabilities: (1) probability of energy state of a neutron (highly simplified to a binary 'fast' or 'slow'), (2) the direction of motion, and (3) the distance to the next collision (Metropolis, 1987). The result was capable of accurately calculating neutron transport through various materials. Mathematically, this was a diabolical problem, so when the Monte Carlo method demonstrated sound results, it significantly moved forward the field of nuclear physics.

Since Fermi's time, computers have greatly enhanced the utility of the Monte Carlo method. As a result, the Monte Carlo research method spread across several research disciplines and industries. In doing so, the Monte Carlo method gathered an assortment of names such as computational economics, agent-based modelling, agent-based complex systems, and individual based modelling. This work uses the term 'ABM'.

The first steps in social science simulation occurred in the 1960s with microanalytic simulation, or microsimulation (Gilbert & Troitzsch, 2005). The key difference between microsimulation and ABMs is that microsimulation designs its agents to act according to empirical data (Bae, Paik, Kim, Singh, & Sajjad, 2016) while pure ABMs seek to find a set of simple rules that give rise to the empirical patterns. Modellers of microsimulations begin with known data and flows without needing to know the underlying cause of the empirical data and trends. These models are perhaps best suited to discovering the systemic outcomes of different circumstances in a system populated by agents operating within empirically established bounds. In this sense, microsimulation may be seen as a closer cousin to system dynamics than to ABMs. An example of an economic microsimulation is Pryor, Basu, and Quint's (1996) model of a simple economy. The key success reported in Pryor et al.'s paper was the reproduction of endogenous business cycles.

Brian Arthur is among the economic pioneers of ABM research. One of his first complexity papers examines how certain technologies become dominant because of their place in history rather than their comparative

(Arthur, 1989). Other groundbreaking work was done by and Axtell who built the famous *Sugarscape* model (Epstein , 1996). *Sugarscape* is a simple model based on an environment consisting of varied quantities of a resource distributed throughout an environment populated by agents harvesting and consuming that resource.

Neither of these last two models attempted to capture the complexity of a modern economy. However, this changed as computers and agent-based modelling platforms become increasingly accessible. Now there exist several papers reporting results from complex macroeconomic ABMs exploring established questions from mainstream and heterodox economics. Some are hybrid models such as Caiani et al.'s (2016) stock-flow consistent Post Keynesian model featuring heterogeneous agents. Others seek to capture phenomena such as endogenous shocks (Dosi et al. 2015; Raberto, Teglio & Cincotti, 2011).

The detailed workings of these types of models are complex and somewhat opaque to economists not involved in ABM research, and sometimes opaque even for other ABM researchers. One academic noted that economic agent-based modellers frequently do not know why their own models act the way they do. 'Mine does this, what does yours do?' he would joke.

The experiments in this book are specifically designed to help us understand the underlying patterns that can appear in even the most complex system models.

4.2   Two Types of Agent-Based Models

Broadly speaking, there are two ways to construct an ABM. One has previously been classed as microsimulation, where empirical data are used to guide the behaviour of, and the links between, agents and other constructs within the simulation. In these types of models, additional or more precise empirical detail is considered beneficial to the model construction. This process results in large complex system models (e.g. Axtell et al., 2014; Caiani et al., 2016; Dosi, Fagiolo, Napoletano, & Roventini, 2013; Dosi, Fagiolo, & Roventini 2010; Raberto, Teglio & Cincotti, 2011; Turrell, 2016).

The goal of these models is frequently empirical prediction. This is, of course, where the big rewards reside. Whoever comes up with the best predictive model can charge huge sums, especially if it involves a lucrative trading market. However, even a moderately successful predictive model is not a good tool to investigate the core behaviour of trade. A detailed accurate ABM is as hard to understand as the reality it is modelling. To understand the nature of trade in a complex system, we need something entirely different.

The second type of model is one designed to specifically understand the complex processes that are occurring within systems. These types of models tend to be very simple, at least in the beginning. The construction of emergent models frequently utilises two or three highly simplified rules to control their agents. Models using this technique have made breakthroughs in their field, such as those featured in Fermi's FERMIAC machine (Metropolis, 1987) and Turchin, Currie, Turner, and Gavrilets' (2013) simulation. In these types of models, the goal is simplicity rather than attempts to capture all imaginable detail and behaviour. As Railsback and Grimm (2011, p. 8) suggest in their guide to programming ABMs, 'We have to force ourselves to simplify as much as we can, or even more'.

Compare the simplicity of Reynolds (1987) model of flocking birds to all the possible detail necessary to accurately model individual flying birds. Each bird will have different flying potential governed by such things as age, strength, ability, and injuries. Individual birds will also be affected by such things as gusts of wind and position in the flock. Is the bird stressed because of interaction with other birds, or because a near miss from a predator? All these facts, and many more, influence the empirical fight patterns of each individual bird. Yet, all these factors were excluded from the successful model. Reynolds demonstrated that programming agents with three simple rules of movement can lead to the same majestic flocking behaviour we see in nature. In doing so, he discovered the core rules governing flocking and schooling behaviour. These same rules are now used to predict the behaviour of people.

In emergent models, accurate empirical detail can be a camouflage covering key underlying rules. By starting with an unrealistically simple model, the researcher can understand how each piece impacts the model when it is added.

In a deleted 2016 blog, the economist Narayana Kocherlakota suggested that simple models, 'toy models' in his words, were more likely to advance macroeconomics than ones attempting to model everything. Going even further back, Von Neumann and Morgenstern (1953, p. 7) state, 'We believe that it is necessary to know as much as possible about [...] the simplest forms of exchange'. That is where this research begins.

The models used for this work are not the first attempt to model the economy using an ABM. They are certainly not the most sophisticated, instead being proudly simplistic. Nor do they attempt to improve on the quantitative accuracy or accurate detailed construction of previous ABMs. The model used most frequently in this work is so simple that it can be fully described in a single paragraph of prose. Like Reynolds' breakthrough model, the models are designed to reveal what emerges from the most basic rules of trade in a complex system.

A search was done to find previous ABM work establishing the foundational complexity forces of trade in monetary systems generally, and fitness functions specifically. There is some notable work done in the distribution of money in a dynamic trade system (Dragulescu & Yakovenko, 2000). There is some basic trade network research done by Wilhite (2001) and some foundational research into barter trade done by Epstein and Axtell (1996), but neither of these latter two works involves fiat money in their models. On the other hand, there is the Minority Game model (Challet & Zhang, 1997) whose principles are used as a foundation to create highly regarded trading market simulations (Gou, 2006). While some of these models are built with evolutionary prerequisites, I could find no work specifically identifying the prerequisites as an evolutionary fitness function and its implications.

This failure to find research is not definitive. Much of the early ABM work remains as obscure working papers or talks (Tesfatsion, 2002, Footnote 3). Also, while agent-based modelling is currently a fringe activity in academic economics, researchers outside have been busy investigating the economy using this key complexity tool (e.g. Foley, 2013; Sinha & Chakrabarti, 2009; Turrell, 2016). It is possible that some foundation emergent research has been done but is either too obscure or so deep in industry or another academic discipline to find in a reasonable time.

4.3   AGENT-BASED MODELLING PITFALLS

Despite a decades-long history in science, the debate around best practice in agent-based modelling continues to this day. To help, Barth, Meyer, and Spitzner (2012) did a survey of ABM research, primarily in business management and the military, and found five common ABM research pitfalls. They are the:

1. distraction pitfall
2. complexity pitfall
3. implementation pitfall
4. interpretation pitfall
5. acceptance pitfall.

The distraction pitfall comes from the ease of adding elements to an ABM. The idea is that the model can answer more than one question at a time. The problem is that each new element adds to the complexity of the output and it becomes increasingly difficult to know what is causing the patterns of interest. Barth et al. (2012, paragraph 2.4) suggest that the drive towards too much complexity can come from many sources:

> In a business environment as well as in the armed forces, clients or superiors might request to have several questions addressed in one model. In science, similar pressures might be exerted from fellow scientists in an audience, supervisors, reviewers, etc. Inexperienced modellers can succumb to believing that they are "not accomplishing enough" in the project. (Barth et al., 2012, paragraph 2.4)

The complexity pitfall is somewhat related to the distraction pitfall. The ease at which realistic elements can be added is beguiling and can lead a modeller, especially a new modeller, to create something so close to reality that it becomes just as difficult to interpret.

> It is a balancing act between simplifying and exact representation. However, going too much in the direction of exact representation of the target system bears the risk of drowning in details and losing sight of the big picture. The resulting model structure becomes increasingly complex and comprehensive. Sometimes this complexity even causes a simulation project to fail. We call this the complexity pitfall. (Barth et al., 2012, paragraph 2.5).

The implementation pitfall relates to a researcher's choice of modelling infrastructure. For example, at the time of writing, the multi-agent programming platform, Netlogo (Wilensky, 1999), uses only a single computer core. As such, the model cannot be scaled up through networking with other computers. If a modeller wanted to test a complex social simulation populated by a full 7 billion agents, for example, Netlogo would not allow it. The researcher would have to weigh the disadvantages of being restricted to much smaller populations. If the disadvantages are not acceptable, then Netlogo would not be a suitable choice for a multi-agent programming platform.

The interpretation pitfall involves a researcher's over-validation of their model's results, primarily as a result of losing a critical distance from their model.

> Losing critical distance to the simulation results can be responsible for undiscovered model errors or reduced efforts in validation. It also has to be noted again that a model is a simplified representation of reality that can only yield valid results for the context it was originally created for. Going beyond that context means to lose the results' validity and can lead to improper or even false conclusions. It happens for example when the analyzed aspect is not part of the reality represented by the model or when the model is too simple and does not allow for valid interpretations. These wrong conclusions resulting from a loss of critical distance is what we call the interpretation pitfall. (Barth et al., 2012, paragraph 2.9)

The acceptance pitfall is the rejection of valid simulation results by third-party gate-keepers. 'In many settings, third-party decision-makers have the final word and hardly know the model. The more distant they are to the modelling process and the more complex the simulation model is, the more sceptical they tend to be about the results' (Barth et al., 2012, paragraph 2.11).

The acceptance pitfall is particularly frustrating when a modeller is investigating new areas and making discoveries that counter accepted wisdom. One reason decision-makers become interested in agent-based modelling lies in its potential to reveal new aspects to old problems. This new-found interest is frequently maintained only if the exciting new aspects do not conflict with accepted wisdom. As Barth et al. (2012, paragraph 2.11) put it: 'A related observation is that doubts are to be raised particularly in situations in which the results do not meet the expectations of third-party decision makers'.

Along with all the above five pitfalls, Barth et al. (2012) make the following suggestions to overcome them:

1. **Distraction Pitfall**—Articulate the question at hand and stay focused on it. This helps keep the part of reality to be modelled manageable.

2. **Complexity Pitfall**—Look for possibilities to simplify your model in order to prevent the simulation from putting its tractability and analysis at risk.
3. **Implementation Pitfall**—Choose the IT implementation based on the model structure at hand rather than based on existing IT systems to avoid restrictions and complications for the IT realisation.
4. **Interpretation Pitfall**—Critically analyze simulation behaviour and scrutinize its results to avoid wrong conclusions.
5. **Acceptance Pitfall**—Avoid the impression of simulation as a 'black box' and consider the experience of your audience to increase acceptance when you communicate your results (Barth et al., 2012, paragraph 3.27).

4.4   THE 'MODEL TUNING' CRITICISM

Some researchers have complained to me that ABMs can be 'tuned' by researchers to create outcomes that support the researcher's narrative. While it is important to report the boundary behaviour of models where relevant, tuning a model for realism is much like Max Planck tuning his energy equation ($E = hv$; where E is energy, v is frequency, h is the Planck constant) by inserting a constant to make the results fit reality (McEvoy & Zarate, 2014). When Planck reported his result, he did not present all the outcomes of his energy equation using all possible real numbers as a constant—he only presented the one that worked. Nor did researchers dismiss Planck's energy equation because it only worked with one constant. Furthermore, even Planck himself did not know what his own constant meant for physics; that was discovered later, especially as Planck himself refused to accept the implications of his successful equation.

The precise settings that cause empirical trends to emerge from an ABM are significant in the same way, though not always with the same magnitude of significance, as the Planck Constant. Also, like the Planck Constant, presenting all possible outcomes of an ABM would take years on small models and generations on big models. Even were someone to do so, who would read them? As you are about to see, even the simplest models, as the one used in the bulk of this paper, can have a huge range of possible configurations. Key trends, findings, and failures are presented rather than describing all possible configurations. If a reader has a yearning to explore a dimension that was not presented here, the models are freely available (see the appendices). It would literally take volumes of books to describe all the testing that has taken place that has gone into this research.

On the other hand, it is also important not to over-represent results, especially if the experimenter has done limited simulation runs. For this work, hundreds and sometimes thousands of runs have been done in each configuration in the search for deviations from the norm. Any significant deviations are reported in the text.

REFERENCES

Arthur, W. (1989). Competing technologies, increasing returns, and lock-in by historical events. *The Economic Journal, 99*(394), 116–131.

Axtell, R., Farmer, D., Geanakoplos, J., Howitt, P., Carrella, E., Conlee, B., ... Palmer, N. (2014). *An agent-based model of the housing market bubble in metropolitan Washington, DC.* New York: Mimeo (George Mason University, Oxford University, Yale University and Brown University).

Bae, J. W., Paik, E., Kim, K., Singh, K., & Sajjad, M. (2016). Combining microsimulation and agent-based model for micro-level population dynamics. *Procedia Computer Science, 80*, 507–517.

Barth, R., Meyer, M., & Spitzner, J. (2012). Typical pitfalls of simulation modeling-lessons learned from armed forces and business. *Journal of Artificial Societies and Social Simulation, 15*(2), 5. http://jasss.soc.surrey. ac.uk/15/2/5.html.

Caiani, A., Godin, A., Caverzasi, E., Gallegati, M., Kinsella, S., & Stiglitz, J. E. (2016). Agent based-stock flow consistent macroeconomics: Towards a benchmark model. *Journal of Economic Dynamics and Control, 69*, 375–408.

Challet, D., & Zhang, Y. C. (1997). Emergence of cooperation and organization in an evolutionary game. *Physica A: Statistical Mechanics and its Applications, 246*(3–4), 407–418.

Dosi, G., Fagiolo, G., Napoletano, M., & Roventini, A. (2013). Income distribution, credit and fiscal policies in an agent-based Keynesian model. *Journal of Economic Dynamics and Control, 37*(8), 1598–1625.

Dosi, G., Fagiolo, G., Napoletano, M., Roventini, A., & Treibich, T. (2015). Fiscal and monetary policies in complex evolving economies. *Journal of Economic Dynamics and Control, 52*, 166–89.

Dosi, G., Fagiolo, G., & Roventini, A. (2010). Schumpeter meeting Keynes: A policy-friendly model of endogenous growth and business cycles. *Journal of Economic Dynamics and Control, 34*(9), 1748–1767.

Dragulescu, A., & Yakovenko, V. M. (2000). Statistical mechanics of money. *The European Physical Journal B-Condensed Matter and Complex Systems, 17*(4), 723–729.

Epstein, J., & Axtell, R. (1996). *Growing artificial societies: Social sciences from the bottom up.* Cambridge: MIT Press.

Foley, S. (2013, October 18). Physicists and the financial markets. *FT Magazine* (online). https://www.ft.com/content/8461f5e6-35f5-11e3-952b-00144fe-ab7de.

Gilbert, N., & Troitzsch, K. (2005). *Simulation for the social scientist.* Oxford: Oxford University Press.

Gou, C. (2006). The simulation of the financial markets by an agent based mix-game model. *Journal of Artificial Societies and Social Simulation, 9*(3). http://jasss.soc.surrey.ac.uk/9/3/6.html.

McEvoy, J. P., & Zarate, O. (2014). *Introducing quantum theory: A graphic guide.* London: Icon Books.

Metropolis, N. (1987). The beginning of the Monte Carlo method. *Los Alamos Science Special Issue, 15,* 125–130. http://permalink.lanl.gov/object/tr?what=info:lanl-repo/lareport/LA-UR-88-9067.

Pryor, R. J., Basu, N., & Quint, T. (1996). Development of Aspen: A microanalytic simulation model of the US Economy (SAND96-0434). Sandia National Laboratories.

Railsback, S. F., & Grimm, V. (2011). *Agent-based and individual-based modeling: A practical introduction.* Princeton university press.

Raberto, M., Teglio, A., & Cincotti, S. (2011). *Debt deleveraging and business cycles: An agent-based perspective.* Economics Discussion Paper (2011–31).

Reynolds, C. (1987). Flocks, herds and schools: A distributed behaviour model. *Computer Graphics, 21*(4), 25–34.

Sinha, S., & Chakrabarti, B. K. (2009). Towards a physics of economics. *Physics News (Bulletin of Indian Physics Association), 39*(2), 33–46.

Tesfatsion, L. (2002). Agent-based computational economics: Growing economies from the bottom up. *Artificial life, 8*(1), 55–82.

Turchin, P., Currie, T., Turner, E., & Gavrilets, S. (2013, September 23). War, space, and the evolution of Old World societies. In *Proceedings of the National Academy of Sciences of the United States of America.* https://doi.org/10.1073/pnas.1308825110. http://www.pnas.org/content/early/2013/09/20/1308825110.

Turrell, A. (2016) *Agent-based models: Understanding the economy from the bottom up.* Quarterly Bulletin 2016 Q4, Bank of England. http://www.bank-ofengland.co.uk/publications/Pages/quarterlybulletin/2016/q4/a2.aspx.

Von Neumann, J., & Morgenstern, O. (1953). *Theory of games and economic behavior* (3rd ed.). Princeton: Princeton University Press.

Wilensky, U. (1999). NetLogo. http://ccl.northwestern.edu/netlogo/. Center for Connected Learning and Computer-Based Modeling. Northwestern University, Evanston, IL.

Wilhite, A. (2001). Bilateral trade and 'small-world' networks. *Computational Economics, 18*(1), 49–64.

CHAPTER 5

Netlogo

Abstract Netlogo is the most common language used to introduce students to multi-agent models. It was designed by academics as a teaching and research tool. While some experienced academics consider Netlogo much like a bicycle with its training wheels still attached, Netlogo offers the advantage of allowing anyone with a personal computer to run and modify these models. This chapter offers a brief overview of how Netlogo works in order to understand the experiments later in the book.

Keywords Netlogo · Agent-based modelling · User manual · Download link · Patches · Agents · Random number generator · Netlogo charts

This is an overview chapter for those new Netlogo (Wilensky, 1999), not an attempt at a full description. Near the end of this section, there is some technical information about Netlogo's integer range and pseudo-random number generator. The full Netlogo's user manual is freely available online at http://ccl.northwestern.edu/Netlogo/docs/.

Netlogo was developed as an accessible programming language descended from older multi-agent programming environments called StarLogo and Logo. Today, it is widely used in academia, especially as a tool to introduce and teach agent-based modelling.

© The Author(s) 2019   37
T. Gooding, *Economics for a Fairer Society*,
https://doi.org/10.1007/978-3-030-17020-2_5

In simple terms, Netlogo generates an environment and then populates it with agents. By convention, this is called the setup. Once the simulation starts, the agents move and interact with each other and the environment according to the programming. Unless programmed otherwise, the agents will be placed in the environment randomly at the start. This means that the simulation is effectively never at an identical starting point unless forced by the programmer. Similarly, by default, the order in which the agents take their turns is randomised on every iteration. This ensures that outcomes are not artefacts of specific beginning points or a specific order.

5.1   Netlogo Agents and Environment

In this work, Netlogo programs utilise environments and agents. The environment in Netlogo is made up of patches. The patches are square. Each patch can contain different variables representing environmental characteristics, such as different levels of raw resources. When the patches are programmed to be various colours, they can be individually seen as in Fig. 5.1. There are two very small agents in Fig. 5.1, both programmed to look like people.

Fig. 5.1   Patches with two agents

Agents are objects in the program that represent such things as people or businesses. As a result of its teaching heritage, Netlogo agents are referred to as 'turtles' in its default programming. In reading Netlogo code, it is not unusual to see something like 'ask turtles' which means 'ask all moving agents to do something'.

The turtle reference makes a useful distinction in the models as both patches and agents can act as individuals. For example, a patch can be programmed to act like a 'brick and mortar' shop. The key difference between a patch and a turtle is that the latter can move while the former cannot. Therefore, the full set of agents will include all turtles and any patches programmed to act as non-moving agents.

Movement is created by changing an agent's position in the environment. Figure 5.2 shows a close-up of an agent and 25 patches. If that agent moves 2 patch lengths in a 90-degree direction, the agent travels right two patch lengths, stopping on the last patch to its right.

Economic-simulated environments generally use one of two topologies. When the environment edge acts as a boundary to movement, it is called a bounded topology. This might be useful if one is trying to

Fig. 5.2   One agent in a 5 × 5 patch environment

simulate an open system, such as a country or a section of a domestic economy. On the other hand, if one is experimenting with the world dynamics, then a closed system topology is needed. In such an environment, if an agent travels off one edge of the environment, it reappears on the opposite edge. This is called a toroidal topology. For example, if Fig. 5.2 features a 5 × 5 patch toroidal topology and the agent moves 4 patch lengths straight upwards (0 degree), it will come to rest one patch below its current position.

It should be noted that not all ABMs require a functional environment. Neither the Simple Economy model featured in Section 7.1 nor Caiani et al.'s (2016) stock-flow consistent simulation requires a simulated physical space in which their agents can move.

Agent movement is not tied to patches. Patches are a loose method to locate the agent (there are specific coordinates which can be accessed) and patch lengths are simply an internally consistent measure of length. One patch length equals the distance from the middle of one patch to the middle of an adjacent patch. The agent can move in any direction to fractional degrees and any distance. They need not move from the middle of one patch to the middle of another. A 1-patch-length move at 45 degrees would land the agent on the same patch if it began the movement on the extreme lower left of a single patch. Regardless, the distance travelled is usually stated as being 'one patch'.

5.2   Brief Overview of Basic Netlogo Processes

Both patches and agents can carry as many or as few variables as the programmer wishes. The variables are then acted upon by the program itself. For example, if one agent seeks the lowest price to make a purchase, the program will ask the buying agent to search within a prescribed area (the entire environment, agents on a neighbouring patch, or the nearest agent, depending on the programming) for all agents possessing goods (their goods variable is >0) and then compare the selling price (the variable holding the current selling price asked by the seller) of the goods until it finds the lowest price. A sale will be an adjustment of the variables of the trading agents. The quantity of purchased goods will be subtracted from the seller's variable tracking the good's ownership and added to the buyer's good's variable. Similarly, money will be subtracted from the buyer and added to the seller. If bank accounts are involved, then possibly, four agents will be included in the transactions (buyer, seller, bank-of-buyer, and bank-of-seller).

Most good economic agent-based models will be 'stock-flow consistent', meaning that there are no undue leaks in goods, money, or energy (if applicable). On the other hand, a program might consider such things as wear and tear and/or consumption of goods, and money leakages such as torn or otherwise destroyed or lost notes/bills.

The combination of agent variables, patch variables, and a program prescribing how the variables interact is extremely flexible. It can usefully represent almost any system made up of multiple agents, whether they are the same type of agents, such as flocks of birds or a crowd of people, or a system populated by a variety of agents such as banks, businesses, people, and governments.

Most Netlogo models have iteration counters. Usually, the iteration counter counts the number of times all agents and patches have once implemented all their instructions. For example, if a program solely consists of asking all agents to move forward 1 patch in a random direction, then once all agents have moved forward 1 patch, an iteration is completed. On the second iteration, all agents will move forward 1 patch again. This is repeated for each iteration until the program is stopped. In this example, after 10 iterations, all agents will have made 10 moves each.

5.3   Netlogo Random Number Generator

Netlogo uses a pseudo-random number generator called the Mersenne Twister (Matsumoto & Nishimura, 1998) that was coded by Luke (2010). This is used whenever probabilities or randomness are invoked and used to do such basic procedures such as determining the order in which the agents will take their turns. The random number generator can be manually seeded using integers that range from −2,147,483,648 to 2,147,483,647. If a probability is calculated as whole numbers, such as 'random 100', the single number returned will be in the inclusive range of 0–99.

The last reported error-free integer range of Netlogo is −2,147,483,648 to 2,147,483,647. Netlogo can run much larger numbers with small errors creeping in, but these errors generally do not interfere with the dynamics of the system. In version 6.0 of Netlogo, graphs stop graphing when variables reach approximately 1 e19. On models where this is expected to happen, there is an automatic simulation stop when the (expected) largest variable reaches 8 e18.

Recently, a Netlogo program of mine crashed because it attempted and failed to complete this operation: 1.7850287151772617 e308 × 1.0101. That means that the program successfully processed 1.7850287151772617 e308 before there was an attempt to increase that number.

5.4   Netlogo Graphs

Most of the graphs used in this work are generated in Netlogo. In agent-based models, the most significant outcome is frequently the graph pattern, not the quantitative result. Accordingly, Netlogo graphs do not contain a great deal of quantitative information.

It is important to note that the numbers on the axes indicate the extent to which the graph background is visible, not the minimum or maximum of the graph within. Netlogo graphs automatically adjust both the x and y axes to accommodate the largest numbers graphed, compressing the graph to fit.

For example, consider two graphs (Fig. 5.3) showing increasing evolutionary fitness of RobbyGA (n.d.), a model described in Chapter 6.

A cursory glance could lead to the mistaken belief that the left and right graphs are quite similar. However, the top y-axes numbers are 368 and 72.8, respectively. The statistics for these two lines in the graphs are: left graph → max 344, mean 288; right graph → max 66, mean 57.

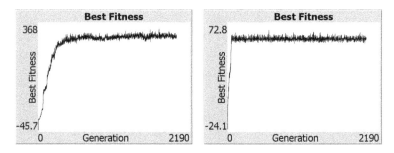

Fig. 5.3 Two graphs of evolutionary fitness

While pattern similarity is frequently more significant than the quantitative outcome, sometimes there are important differences in magnitudes.

REFERENCES

Caiani, A., Godin, A., Caverzasi, E., Gallegati, M., Kinsella, S., & Stiglitz, J. E. (2016). Agent based-stock flow consistent macroeconomics: Towards a benchmark model. *Journal of Economic Dynamics and Control, 69*, 375–408.

Luke, S. (2010). The ECJ owner's manual. *San Francisco, California, A User Manual for the ECJ Evolutionary Computation Library*, 1–206.

Matsumoto, M., & Nishimura, T. (1998). Mersenne twister: A 623-dimensionally equidistributed uniform pseudo-random number generator. *ACM Transactions on Modeling and Computer Simulation (TOMACS), 8*(1), 3–30.

RobbyGA. (n.d.). *"Robby the robot genetic algorithms" model, complexity explorer project.* http://complexityexplorer.org.

Wilensky, U. (1999). *Netlogo*. Evanston, IL: Center for Connected Learning and Computer-Based Modeling, Northwestern University. http://ccl.northwestern.edu/Netlogo/.

CHAPTER 6

Evolution in Netlogo

Abstract Wherever less successful heterogeneous people try to emulate those more successful, evolution will result. We know this because these are prerequisites for evolutionary systems. Similar prerequisites are routinely used by scientists, engineers, and industry to create specified parts and systems. What will arise from the resulting evolutionary forces is not always self-evident. This is where agent-based model experiments are most useful. This describes precisely how to place the prerequisites of evolution into a multi-agent economic model and demonstrates some results.

Keywords Evolution · Evolutionary prerequisites · Evolutionary outcomes · Evolutionary fitness · Starvation · Agent-based models · Netlogo

Evolution is a specific form of emergent behaviour (emergence over time). We already know that group behaviour can be predicted by using the principles of emergent behaviour (Bonabeau, 2002; Challenger, Clegg, & Robinson, 2009). Today, emergent models are used to predict how crowds will move at events such as the Notting Hill Carnival (Batty, DeSyllas, & Duxbury, 2003) and to understand traffic patterns (Kerner, 2012). The military use it to determine the outcome of a number of scenarios (Barth, Meyer, & Spitzner, 2012). Some models use evolutionary emergence to reproduce key societal trends or historical patterns.

© The Author(s) 2019
T. Gooding, *Economics for a Fairer Society*,
https://doi.org/10.1007/978-3-030-17020-2_6

For example, Turchin, Currie, Turner & Gavrilets' (2013) model captures the empirical rise of ancient civilizations over 3000 years in Africa, Asia, and Europe. Accordingly, unless the free market is scientifically unique, emergence will shape the economy just as it shapes crowds and society. This is especially true in markets possessing evolutionary prerequisites.

Evolutionary systems are so predictable that engineers and scientists use them to design and build hardware and software (Greenwood & Tyrrell, 2006). To my knowledge, no system possessing evolutionary prerequisites has failed to evolve. The necessary evolutionary prerequisites are empirically observable in markets and in society. As we will see, when these same prerequisites are placed in agent-based models, empirical patterns emerge.

The following prerequisites will trigger evolutionary processes: (1) heterogeneous agents and (2) less successful agents imitating more successful agents. It is self-evident that people and businesses are heterogeneous. Similarly, a search reveals countless seminars, books, talks, online videos, etc., offering to reveal the habits and practices of those who are already rich. The market indicates a strong desire of people to imitate success. Any system with these prerequisites will evolve in a very specific manner. As we will see, capturing evolutionary prerequisites in agent-based models is trivial.

6.1   GENETIC ALGORITHMS

One accepted type of evolutionary algorithm is called the genetic algorithm (GA), as exemplified by a model in the Netlogo model library called Simple Genetic Algorithm (Stonedahl & Wilensky, 2008). The GA is initiated with a population of randomly generated agents which then perform a task and is then scored according to the fitness function. The agents are then ranked so the top-ranked performers can be identified. The high performers are pair up and parts of their instruction code combined (and sometimes mutated), and the result populates the next generation. The old generation is removed, and the cycle begins again.

An example of this is Robby the Robot (Mitchell, Tisue, & Wilensky 2012), a Netlogo program used to demonstrate the GA. The specific version used here comes from the Santa Fe Institute (RobbyGA, n.d.)

There is a version of Robby the Robot available in the Netlogo model library that comes with the Netlogo download. Quoting from the 'info' tab in the RobbyGA simulator,

> Robby the Robot is a virtual robot who moves around a room and picks up cans. This model demonstrates the use of a genetic algorithm (GA) to evolve control strategies for Robby. The GA starts with randomly generated strategies and then uses evolution to improve them. (see RobbyGA. nlogo 'Info' tab)

The room is a bounded topology consisting of a 10×10 grid and randomly populated by garbage cans. The agent can 'see' what's on their grid (or patch) and the four grids immediately next to them in the cardinal four directions (not the diagonal). The evolutionary fitness is determined by how many cans an agent picks up without making false moves, such as trying to move outside the bounded topology or trying to pick up a can where there is none. A population of 100 (a user-adjustable number) agents, each with randomly generated strategies, all take turns within this environment. During each iteration, the 100 agents apply their strategy in 20 different randomly generated environments and their fitness averaged. At the end of each iteration, the top 15 fittest agents are selected to reproduce the new generation before the old population is removed.

Figure 6.1 depicts graphs from two simulation runs of RobbyGA. They depict iterations (time) on the x-axis and the fitness of the fittest agent in the system on the y-axis. The graph on the left is 1500 or 1500

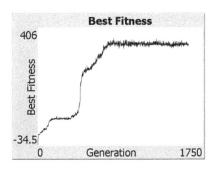 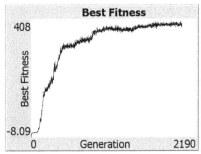

Fig. 6.1   Two runs of RobbyGA

generations, and the graph on the right is 2000 iterations. The graphs in Fig. 5.3 are also from this simulation.

While the evolutionary path differs in each case, both systems experience the same pressure to improve fitness, even if the fitness gets stuck at a certain level as it does briefly in left graph of Fig. 5.3. Note that as the iterations increase, the probability of improvement increases.

6.2   EVOLUTION BY CIRCUMSTANCE

Genetic algorithms are highly prescribed. Reality is more fluid. Accordingly, the GA is modified to more closely reflect reality in the following manner:

- Agents are given a lifetime of 7 iterations after which they die. Agents are initiated with random ages so only a percentage of the population dies of 'old age' during each iteration.
- A percentage of poorly performing agents are killed. The cause of death is arbitrarily called 'starvation', but it could also be called 'bankruptcy' or, something/someone from culture being 'forgotten'.
- Whenever the population falls below the initial 100, random agents are paired up to create new agents. The parental agents share and mutate their code when they breed as they did in the GA.
- Any surviving agent can reproduce, regardless of their evolutionary fitness.

This set-up was run for 3000 iterations with a starvation rate of 30%. This means that 30% of the lowest-performing agents are removed each iteration. After 3000 iterations, the starvation rate is set to 0, meaning no one dies except from old age. At the 6000-iteration mark, starvation is reintroduced at 30%. This cycle is repeated until the simulation is stopped at 16,000 iterations. The result (Fig. 6.2) clearly shows the impact of evolutionary forces. A vertical line running from −50 to 350 marks the fitness function transition points. The horizontal line is zero.

It should be noted that simulation runs of this nature are not always so neat. When the fitness function is switched off, the system sometimes

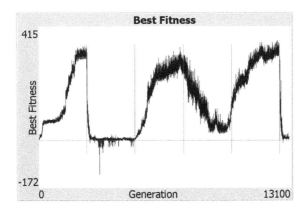

Fig. 6.2 Fitness function switched on and off every 3000 iterations

continues to climb in fitness for a time. However, as more time goes by, it becomes increasingly likely that the fitness will fall.

On the other hand, as in Fig. 6.3, a system under evolutionary pressure can sometimes get stuck at a low level for a time. However, the longer an evolutionary simulation is run, the more probable it becomes that agent fitness will rise. The evolutionary pressure is always there.

The tables below record the final best fitness from 2 sets of 20 simulation runs ending at 3000 iterations. The first 20 runs are done with no starvation (Table 6.1). The second set of 20 runs has 'starvation' set to 30% (Table 6.2).

Fig. 6.3 Starvation set to 5%, 10,000 iterations

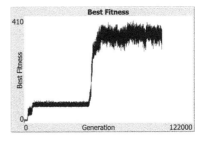

Table 6.1   Starvation set to 0

Average 15.44		Std Dev 21.34		Maximum 70		Minimum −21.25	
−21.25	2.5	27.5	12.5	60	2.5	15	0
17.5	2.5	45	20	5	0	5	11.25
15	70	10	8.75				

Table 6.2   Starvation set to 30%

Average 205.11		Std Dev 82.38		Maximum 277.5		Minimum 67.5	
67.5	205	67.5	245	258.75	67.5	227.5	72.5
243.75	252.5	250	263.75	266.25	233.75	273.75	273.75
277.5	238.5	247.5	70				

6.3   Evolutionary Strength

This is a term developed for this work. As will be demonstrated, the strength of evolutionary systems can vary. As a result, depending on the evolutionary strength, different patterns can emerge with the same fitness test. In the real world, it is possible to have several measures of evolutionary fitness in the same system. As their various evolutionary strengths rise and fall, the overall system could experience shifts in dominant fitness tests leading to different outcomes even though all other things are equal.

The strength is determined by setting how aggressive the system disempowers poor performers and/or empowers the most successful. Engineers and scientists using evolutionary processes to achieve particular outcomes tend to use aggressive settings. For example, in a genetic algorithm (a particular type of artificial evolutionary system), it is typical to weed out 90% or more of the less capable performers with respect to the fitness function. However, one of the first to write about targeted evolutionary system (Hillis, 1999) only removed agents performing below the mean fitness.

Changing the evolutionary strength can change the overall patterns. However, the evolutionary pressure never changes. For example, if we lower the starvation rate in the example above from 30 to 5%, large plateaus tend to form. On the other hand, sooner or later, the system succumbs to evolutionary pressure (Fig. 6.3). Figure 6.3 features 100,000 iterations, whereas Fig. 6.2 went through three evolutionary cycles in just 16,000 iterations. Time is a great equaliser in evolutionary processes.

REFERENCES

Barth, R., Meyer, M., & Spitzner, J. (2012). Typical pitfalls of simulation modeling-lessons learned from armed forces and business. *Journal of Artificial Societies and Social Simulation, 15*(2), 5. http://jasss.soc.surrey.ac.uk/15/2/5.html.

Batty, M., DeSyllas, J., & Duxbury, E. (2003). The discrete dynamics of small-scale spatial events: Agent-based models of mobility in carnivals and street parades. *International Journal of Geographical Information Science, 17*(7), 673–697.

Bonabeau, E. (2002). Agent-based modeling: Methods and techniques for simulating human systems. *Proceedings of the National Academy of Sciences, 99*(suppl 3), 7280–7287.

Challenger, R., Clegg, C. W., & Robinson, M. A. (2009). Understanding crowd behaviours: Supporting evidence. *Understanding Crowd Behaviours (Crown, 2009)* (pp. 1–326).

Greenwood, G. W., & Tyrrell, A. M. (2006). *Introduction to evolvable hardware: A practical guide for designing self-adaptive systems* (Vol. 5). Hoboken: Wiley.

Hillis, W. D. (1999). *The pattern on the stone: The simple ideas that make computers work*. New York: Basic Books (AZ).

Kerner, B. S. (2012). *The physics of traffic: Empirical freeway pattern features, engineering applications, and theory*. Berlin: Springer.

Mitchell, M., Tisue, S., & Wilensky, U. (2012). *Netlogo 'Robby the Robot' model*. Evanston, IL: Center for Connected Learning and Computer-Based Modeling, Northwestern University. http://ccl.northwestern.edu/Netlogo/models/RobbytheRobot.

RobbyGA. (n.d.). *"Robby the robot genetic algorithms" model, Complexity Explorer project*. http://complexityexplorer.org.

Stonedahl, F., & Wilensky, U. (2008). *Netlogo simple genetic algorithm model*. Evanston, IL: Center for Connected Learning and Computer-Based Modeling, Northwestern University. http://ccl.northwestern.edu/Netlogo/models/SimpleGeneticAlgorithm.

Turchin, P., Currie, T., Turner, E., & Gavrilets, S. (2013, September 23). War, space, and the evolution of Old World societies. In *Proceedings of the National Academy of Sciences of the United States of America*. https://doi.org/10.1073/pnas.1308825110. http://www.pnas.org/content/early/2013/09/20/1308825110.

CHAPTER 7

Verifying Model Results

Abstract Verifying that agent-based model results involve two steps. One is to ensure that the code is sound, and that it is operating according to the experimental design. The second is to ensure that the results are robust and not an artefact of specific code or a particular design. This is a particular challenge when the outcome involves patterns that are not amenable to statistical analysis. This explains steps taken to ensure that the results in this book are robust.

Keywords Code verification · Pattern robustness · Agent-based modelling · Evolution · Emergent behaviour

If the agent-based models are initiated in different states and complex systems are sensitive to initial conditions, then how can we get robust results? What we are looking for are consistent patterns emerging from the general noise of the system—patterns arising from forces created by the rules of the system even when the initial conditions are changed.

Reynolds' (1987) groundbreaking bird-flocking simulations did not attempt to quantify where a particular bird is going to fly, or the average height of a flock after 3 minutes. It simply tried to recreate the same majestic patterns that we see in reality using simple rules of individual behaviour. Similarly, this work applies known market behaviour rules to individual agents to see what emerges.

The validity of the results depends largely on two things. One is to be certain that the model is programmed accurately—that the model is doing what the researcher believes it is doing. This is called verifying the code. An agent-based model is much like a physical experiment, in that if it happens in an agent-based model, it will happen in nature wherever the same prerequisites are present. The only concern is that a program is doing something unbeknownst to the researcher.

Verifying the results involves demonstrating that the results are repeatable, not the result of specific programming or model design. Specifically, to what extent do different simulation configurations and different initial conditions lead to the same or different trends?

Verifying is a time-consuming task and full reporting is difficult as a full write-up of all its glorious detail can take up enormous written space. The following is a brief overview of what has been done to verify the results in this work.

Note that there is no attempt to empirically validate quantitative outcomes, partly because we are seeking patterns, and partly because this is the beginning of this type of research. A lot more research needs to be done even before we know where quantitative empirical prediction of complex-system economics can be accomplished.

7.1   VERIFYING THE CODE

Code is verified in several ways. One is to track the variables held by individual agents to ensure that they change in a rational manner. If an agent sells a product, their money should go up and their supply of goods go down. The buying agent's money should go down while their supply goes up. Furthermore, the sum of these quantities across all the agents in the system should remain unchanged, unless it is programmed to be otherwise.

In the basic Toy Trader model, the agents are only doing one thing—trading toys for money. Accordingly, there are only two practical variables that need tracking: money and toys. Most programming mistakes in this area can be detected by the sum of money and toys deviating from the initial system totals. Accordingly, monitors for these two variables are built into the model interface allowing continual monitoring.

Another way of verifying the code is to program the same procedure in a different way. If behaviour coded in several different ways create similar patterns, we know that the system results are robust. In the models presented here, several coding experiments have been done to find pro-gramming efficiencies. This reveals which outcomes are coding specific and which ones are the result of general systemic forces. This process also serves to ensure that the final programming is robust and free of logical errors.

Another programming habit is to chart variables not directly involved in the experiments. For example, in the Toy Trader model, there are charts tracking maximum toys held by a single agent, minimum toys, the number of extremely poor agents (determined by an ad hoc assumption), and the maximum of money + toys × average price. By tracking all these variables, it is a simple matter to keep an eye on the integrity of the pro-gramme. For example, if the number of toys held by any agent goes to −1 (or less), it necessarily indicates a coding error.

The remainder of this chapter examines the stability of the patterns arising from the Toy Trader model in different settings.

7.2   PATTERN ROBUSTNESS

Broadly speaking, there are two types of runs. While all runs feature sto-chastic processes—the agents are initialised and placed randomly in the environment and they take random turns—configurations without evo-lutionary process are nearly deterministic. In this case, pattern robust-ness can be determined statistically. Evolutionary robustness is tested by the consistency of their patterns, just as with flocking birds. This chapter looks at the non-evolutionary and evolutionary simulation patterns and establishes their robustness for this work.

7.2.1   Non-evolutionary Patterns

Over thousands of runs, the non-evolutionary patterns arising in the models in this work show very close correlations. For example, Fig. 7.1 is the Gini coefficient of a Toy Trader simulation run (see Sect. 8.2). If we do five runs with different starting points and different order of trade, the results demonstrate a very high statistical correlation, as can be seen in Table 7.1.

Table 7.2 is the summary statistics of the 10 correlations in Table 7.1 with the 1's removed (where a line is correlated to itself).

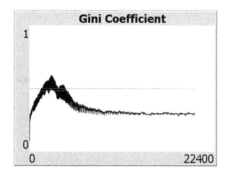

Fig. 7.1   Gini coefficient of a single run to 20,000 iterations

Table 7.1   Correlation of Gini coefficient points between 5 runs where $n = 20,000$

	Run 1	Run 2	Run 3	Run 4	Run 5
Run 1	1				
Run 2	0.9572	1			
Run 3	0.9587	0.9719	1		
Run 4	0.9660	0.9727	0.9756	1	
Run 5	0.9681	0.9512	0.9531	0.9564	1

Table 7.2   Statistic summary of Gini coefficient correlations between 5 runs ($n = 10$)

Mean	Std Dev.	Max.	Min.
0.963094	0.00279	0.975575	0.951194

Figure 7.2 shows a Gini coefficient run at different settings of the Toy Trader model and run to 35,000 iterations. This was chosen because the Gini is relatively dynamic at these settings.

If we correlate 20 runs as we did in Table 7.1, the result is 190 correlations between lines consisting of 35,000 points. Table 7.3 is the statistical summary.

However, these statistics do not convey their general patterns. At these setting, all the Gini coefficients initially pass 0.5 and then fall back.

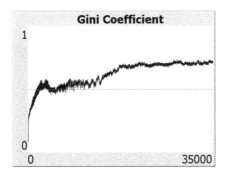

Fig. 7.2   Gini coefficient of a single run to 35,000 iterations

Table 7.3   Statistic summary of Gini coefficient correlations between 20 runs ($n = 180$)

Mean	Std Dev.	Max.	Min.
0.9475	0.0016	0.9765	0.8663

They slowly return to 0.5 before the lines become somewhat chaotic, with some driving upwards and others experiencing shocks. The lines then re-join to march along in their mutual trend. Figure 7.3 shows four of these runs on the same graph. If you look closely, you will also see that there is less noise in the lines after the chaos evident between 15,000 and 23,000 iterations.

While it is possible to mathematically convey these characteristics by dissecting line sections and doing descriptive statistics on the lines and their slopes, it might be the case of where one figure is worth a thousand words.

7.2.2   Evolutionary Patterns

When evolution is invoked, it can make a correlation analysis useless. Consider the price over 6000 iterations of 20 runs of the Toy Trader model. Just as was done with the Gini coefficient in Tables 7.2 and 7.3, price correlations between 20 runs of 6000 iterations are statistically summarised in Table 7.4 ($n = 190$). The results show little statistical significance.

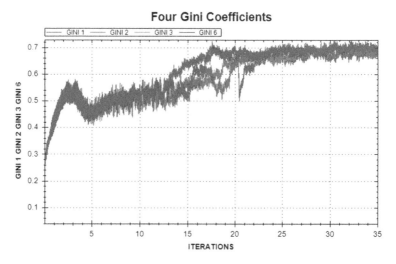

Fig. 7.3   Gini coefficient, 4 runs, 35,000 iterations

Table 7.4   Statistical summary of price correlations between 20 runs ($n = 190$)

Mean	Std Dev.	Max.	Min.
0.276856	0.225483	0.758614	−0.22127

If the prices from those 20 runs are put on the same graph, no unified pattern appears (Fig. 7.4).

In this instance, broad statistical facts are used to demonstrate the difference between runs with different fitness tests. The average price data reported for each iteration are calculated by summing the price of all transactions and dividing by the number of transactions. If we run the above simulation to 6000 iterations, the result will be 6000 pieces of average-price data. If all 6000 iteration prices are summed and averaged over the entire run, a single overall price average is generated.

The simulation is run 100 times to produce a total of 100 pieces of overall average price data. Then the fitness test is changed (see Chapter 10) and another 100 pieces of price data are produced. The result is summarised statistically, and the results are shown in Table 7.5.

Prices in an Evolutionary Run

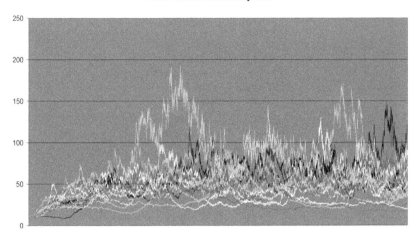

Fig. 7.4 Price, 20 simulation runs, 6000 iterations

Table 7.5 Average price from 100 runs with each fitness test, $n = 100$

	Fitness test 1	Fitness test 2
Mean	45.22	145.29
Median	44.90	144.34
Standard deviation	6.68	9.59
Minimum	31.30	123.69
Maximum	79.67	173.72

Table 7.6 Average price from the final iteration of 100 runs, $n = 100$

	Fitness test 1	Fitness test 2
Mean	56.94	191.84
Median	53.24	189.41
Standard deviation	24.23	13.51
Minimum	21.56	168.59
Maximum	160.77	228.34

The differences are clear. A similar disparity is apparent in the statistics calculated from the average price in the last iteration of 100 runs for each fitness test (Table 7.6).

7.3 SUMMARY

late, runs of the Toy Trader model run at the same settings produce similar patterns. This makes sense as the systemic forces underlying each pattern in the Toy Trader model will not change, even if a strong endogenous shock knocks the system off its normal trajectory.

Readers interested in further pursuing the robustness of the experimental results shown in this work are encouraged to run the simulations for themselves. There will be benefits to doing so as there can be aspects of 'live' simulator performances that are difficult to describe in communications consisting of still images, statistics, and academic prose.

For those interested in more information concerning the verification (or validation) of agent-based models, two recent books cover this topic more in depth (Wilensky & Rand, 2015; Hamill & Gilbert, 2016).

REFERENCES

Hamill, L., & Gilbert, N. (2016). *Agent-based modelling in economics.* Chichester, UK: Wiley.

Reynolds, C. (1987). Flocks, herds and schools: A distributed behaviour model. *Computer Graphics, 21*(4), 25–34.

Wilensky, U., & Rand, W. (2015). *An introduction to agent-based modeling: Modeling natural, social, and engineered complex systems with Netlogo.* Cambridge: MIT Press.

CHAPTER 8

Money Distribution

Abstract Econophysicists have demonstrated that the physical dynamics of monetary trade systems result in a money distribution equal to 0.5 Gini coefficient. This occurs in efficient trade systems where all agents have equal ability and opportunity. The implication is that a market economy does not distribute money based on merit. The Toy Trader model is introduced, and experiments performed are designed to explore this finding and how different trade aspects might impact money distribution.

Keywords Money · Inequality · Distribution · Gini coefficient · Complex system trade · Toy Trader model · Netlogo

What is the starting point of money distribution in a market system? Linear-system theory predicts a meritocracy in perfectly competitive market, but what does complex-system theory predict? This is a key question if we are to build a fair society. If poor people are poor and rich people are rich because of merit, society has little obligation to the poor and while taxing the rich is effectively stealing deserved wealth. However, if wealth is unequally distributed due to the physics of trade, then the picture reverses. Building a fair society will involve buffers against both extreme poverty and extreme wealth to counter systemic forces.

In one of the most-cited inequality papers in economics, Kuznets asks a simple question: 'Does inequality in the distribution of income increase

© The Author(s) 2019
T. Gooding, *Economics for a Fairer Society*,
https://doi.org/10.1007/978-3-030-17020-2_8

or decrease in the course of a country's economic growth?' (Kuznets, 1955, p. 1). In the past, Kuznets was credited with explaining how the free market will lead to less inequality. He was, however, very cautious in his conclusions, noting that his article consists of '5 percent empirical data and 95 percent speculation, some of it possibly tainted by wishful thinking' (ibid., p. 26). He added that the discussion of inequality, in general, consisted of a great deal of strong opinion and just a few facts.

In his paper, Kuznets noted that Karl Marx predicted ever-increasing wealth inequality while living through a time when inequality was increasing. On the other hand, Kuznets predicted decreasing inequality during a time inequality was in decline. By 1992, it had been concluded that 'income is more equally distributed within wealthier countries' (Galor & Zeira, 1993, p. 35) and by 2000, 'Wealth inequality has, on the whole, trended downwards in the twentieth century, although there have been interruptions and reversals' (Davies & Shorrocks, 2000, p. 607).

However, by 2014, what was being recognised as empirical fact had changed. Wealth inequality apparently had risen in most developed countries since the 1970s (Piketty, 2015). Some even suggest that inequality has climbed inexorably since the introduction of agriculture to human society (Kohler et al., 2017).

There is no question that the modern market system has generated a great deal of wealth. However, since 2007 especially, the fairness of distribution has been questioned. However, study of empirical wealth inequality is difficult as noted by Keister (2000, p. ix): 'the lack of data made it nearly impossible to ask many of the questions about wealth to which we would like answers'.

The nature of free-market wealth distribution seems to change from time to time and from writer to writer. This chapter seeks to understand underlying dynamics of the free trade system that do not change whenever historically local data indicate a trend or a change in the trend.

Before we start, try this thought experiment: imagine a room with 500 people in it, each with $100. The sum of all money is $50,000. Then, everyone is asked to give $1 to a random other person in the room, without regard to distance. After everyone has given away $1, the turn ends. The sum of all money remains at $50,000. The question is, after 150,000 turns, how is the money distributed?

One way to describe (in)equality is the Gini coefficient, where a 0 indicates everyone having the same wealth (the starting point of this thought experiment) and 1 is absolute inequality, where one person has all the money. What do you think the outcome of the thought experiment will be in terms of a Gini coefficient?

The Boltzmann–Gibbs distribution was first described by the ninteenth-century physicist Ludwig Boltzmann as a result of studying the energy distribution of gas molecules (Boltzmann, 1965). It is an exponential distribution whereby the sector with the lowest energy potential has the highest population of gas molecules while the highest energy potential has the lowest population. Specifically, the probability distribution of energy, ϵ, is $P(\epsilon) = Ce^{-\epsilon/T}$, where T=temperature and C=a normalising constant (Wannier, 1987).

The econophysicists Dragulescu and Yakovenko (2000) adapted the Boltzmann–Gibbs equation by substituted ϵ for m (money) so that the equation became $P(m) = Ce^{-m/T}$. A series of agent-based model experiments suggest that money distributions in a trading system are likely, over time, to stabilise in a Boltzmann–Gibbs distribution. If true, the core rules governing trade markets mean that a population of agents with equal ability and equal opportunity will end up with an exponential wealth inequality in regard to money. This would be the free market's starting point.

8.1   THE SIMPLE ECONOMY

The Netlogo model, Simple Economy (Wilensky & Rand, 2015), was designed to demonstrate the Boltzmann–Gibbs distribution. It is also the thought experiment given above.

The Simple Economy Model

Population:
- 500 homogeneous agents.

Each agent starts with:
- 100 money.

Each iteration (turn):
- Each agent gives 1 of their money to another randomly chosen agent.

The Boltzmann–Gibbs distribution is a precise description of a system made up of particles with precise behaviour. Human beings are not precise. A tool with this degree of precision may not be ideal for use on groups of people. For economists, a blunter instrument such as the Gini coefficient might more useful for calculating distribution. Therefore, for this paper, a Gini coefficient chart was added to Wilensky and Rand's model. The Gini coefficient goes to 0.5 whenever a Boltzmann–Gibbs distribution is realised, but 0.5 does not guarantee a Boltzmann–Gibbs distribution. Regardless, a 0.5 Gini coefficient does indicate a measurable degree of wealth inequality in the messy world of human beings.

In the Simple Economy simulation, Wilensky and Rand have referred to the items to be traded as 'wealth'. However, wealth might be better called 'money' as Dragulescu and Yakovenko (2000, p. 723) specifically state that '… money is only one part of wealth, the other part being material wealth. Material products have no conservation law […] So, in general, we do not expect the Boltzmann–Gibbs law for the distribution of wealth'. Of course, in the real world, neither money nor goods remain in constant supply. Regardless, to remain clear about the Boltzmann–Gibbs distribution hypothesis, 'wealth' in the Simple Economy will be referred to as 'money'.

All the agents start in the same state, possessing an identical potential. At the start of the simulation, the Gini coefficient is 0. Figure 8.1 is how the simulation appears after 5 iterations. The Gini coefficient is 0.01.

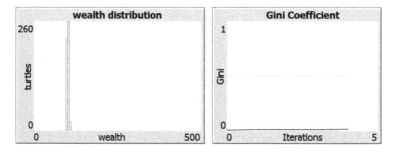

Fig. 8.1   Money distribution after 5 iterations

Graphs

- **Wealth Distribution**—A money distribution histogram in the form of a bar graph. The *y*-axis is the number of agents (labelled as 'turtles' on this graph). The *x*-axis is money. It shows the distribution for the last iteration only.
- **Gini** (chart)—Gini coefficient. On the *y*-axis, 1 is perfect inequality and 0 perfect equality. The *x*-axis is time in iterations. A horizontal reference line is set at 0.50.

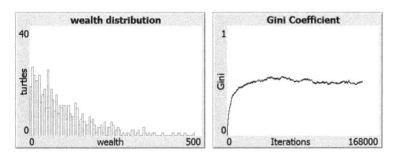

Fig. 8.2 Money distribution after 150,000 iterations

Given the homogeneity of the agents and the identical chance of all agents to receive money, some might intuit that money would remain relatively equally distributed. Figure 8.2 shows the Simple Economy after 150,000 iterations. Note that the Gini coefficient stabilises around 0.5.

8.2 THE TOY TRADER MODEL

As a consumer, once you identify what you want, in most cases, the next most important task is determining where that good or service can be had at the lowest price. As a seller, you adjust your prices according to demand. Many businesses use inventory as a proxy for demand. If the product is not moving or inventory is building up, then the assumption is demand is too low at that price and so price is lowered. If the inventory is rapidly decreasing or keeps running out, raising the price manages the demand and allows the seller to make more money. One simple way to manage inventory is to have an inventory target and use price to maintain it. These are the dynamics that form the basis of the Toy Trader model.

Imagine you are in a 51-metre × 51-metre room containing 400 randomly distributed people. You (and everyone else) are initially given $100 and 5 toys. The price of each toy is initially given at $10 each. First, you (and everyone else) must find the lowest price of a toy within arm's length of yourself. If the lowest available price involves two or more toys priced the same, you randomly pick one. If a toy is available, and you can afford the price, you must purchase one toy. Meanwhile, other people within arm's length will be checking your price to see if your toys are the cheapest in the area. If they are, they will buy from you. Your goal is to use price to reduce and maintain your inventory at 3 toys. After every instance of selling a toy, you check your inventory and, if it is too high (more than 3), you lower your price by multiplying it by 0.99. If it is too low (less than 3), you raise your price by multiplying it by 1.0101. After everyone has tried to purchase one toy, you (like everyone else) turn to face a random direction and move forward one arm's length. This concludes one iteration of the Toy Trader model simulation.

For the runs shown in this chapter, the Toy Trader model uses a population of 400 agents. Each agent is initiated with 100 money and 5 toys. System-wide, the stock of toys and money are fixed and unchanging at 40,000 (400 × 100) money and 2000 (5 × 400) toys.

Initially, 400 agents are randomly placed within a 51 × 51 square toroidal lattice topology, meaning that if someone walks off one edge, they reappear on the opposite side. During each iteration, all agents seek to purchase a single good from another agent at the lowest price they can find forming a demand of 400 toys per iteration. Accordingly, demand is also fixed.

As agents want 3 toys in their inventory in the long-run, overall there are 1200 toys being demanded from a system supply of 2000. The system is in perpetual oversupply. There are no systemic reasons for anyone to become poor.

The Toy Trader Model (Non-evolutionary Configuration)

Population:
• 400 homogeneous agents.

Each agent starts with:
• Money 100.
• Toys 5.
• Toy selling price = 10.

Agent actions:
• Move forward a distance of one patch length in a random (360°) direction.
• Seek to purchase 1 toy at the lowest price within the user-adjustable price detection distance.
• If a toy is sold, check inventory and adjust price (see pricing).

Pricing:
• If, after a sale, toy stock < 3, raise price (price-new = price-old x 1.0101).
• If, after a sale, toy stock > 3, lower price (price-new = price-old x 0.99).
• If, after a sale, toy stock = 3, no change.
• No price change for the buyer after a purchase.

In the Toy Trader model, there are many possible definitions of wealth. This chapter uses three: money only, toys only, or assets (money + toys x average price). This allows us to track three possible wealth distributions in the system to further explore Dragulescu and Yakovenko's claims. The Dragulescu and Yakovenko's paper suggests that if the supply of goods is constant, as is the case in these experiments, all quantities should go to a Boltzmann–Gibbs distribution (0.5 Gini coefficient).

The agents' ability to see other agents' stocks and prices is determined by market-sight, a user-controlled slider that determines the radius in patches that an agent can see. Market-sight = 1 equates to everyone in the room only being able to trade with the people within arm's length. On the other hand, a common assumption in economic models is

Fig. 8.3 Gini coefficient of money, toys, and assets, market-sight = 25, 80,000 iterations

'rational agents', agents that know all prices and can trade with anyone at any time irrespective of distance. To do this in the Toy Trader model, market-sight is set to **25**, a setting where all agents can see all other agents and trade with anyone in the environment. The wealth distribution is tracked in the three categories of wealth, money, toys, and assets. The Gini coefficient for all three can be seen in Fig. 8.3.

Toy Trader Gini Coefficient Graph

- The horizontal reference line set at 0.5.
- Iterations is on the x axis.
- Gini coefficient is on the y axis.

Interestingly, money seems to be much closer to a Boltzmann–Gibbs distribution than either of the other two measures of wealth. One possible explanation for this may lay in Yakovenko's (2016) suggestion that money forms an informational layer in the economy as opposed to a physical layer. If Yakovenko's premise is correct, an economy featuring only one good and money cannot be treated as a barter economy, even if the quantities of both are fixed.

The next step in the experiments is to constrain the agents' ability to see prices by reducing market-sight to 4 (Fig. 8.4). This set-up is also used in Figs. 7.2 and 7.3. At this setting, the agents can detect the prices of goods offered within a 4-patch radius, equivalent to 4 arm's lengths in the room example. At first, it seems that the money distribution

Fig. 8.4 Gini of money, toys, and assets, market-sight = 4, 35,000 iterations

Fig. 8.5 Gini of money, toys, and assets, market-sight = 2, 7300 iterations

does settle down at a Gini coefficient of 0.5. However, as time goes by, the Gini coefficient of money deviates from 0.5. These runs were to 35,000 iterations. After this, the trends stabilise, except for endogenous shocks as exhibited in the last quarter of the Gini coefficient of money.

Next, agents' Market-sight is reduced to a radius of 2 patches. These simulations are run to 7300 iterations (Fig. 8.5).

Money now exhibits a progressive approach towards 0.5 on the Gini coefficient, though it finally stabilises slightly above the predicted level of 0.5. Assets never approach 0.5 while Toys jump towards 0.5 before progressively moving away.

When the market-sight is set to 1, Dragulescu and Yakovenko's claims that everything will go to a 0.5 Gini coefficient are supported as all three Gini charts stabilise within a few points of a 0.5 Gini coefficient (Fig. 8.6).

These initial experiments suggest that econophysicists are partially right about money in a closed trading system taking on a Boltzmann–Gibbs distribution. If agents act as particles or molecules, then the

Fig. 8.6   Gini of money, toys, and assets, market-sight = 1, 15,000 iterations

Fig. 8.7   Money distribution in a complex monetary simulation

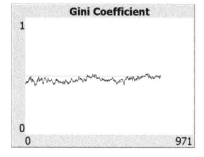

result can look those from thermodynamics and other physical systems. However, agents in an economy can take on many characteristics that deviate from behaviour that can be linked to particles in physics, even in a simulation as simple as the Toy Trader model.

On the other hand, it is evident that the money distribution of a trade economy tends to go towards a 0.5 Gini coefficient. This is tested in the much more complex Metaphoria model (see Chapter 13). Metaphoria features money creation (money is not conserved), production and consumption, jobs, starvation, birth and death, businesses with dividends, and inheritance. The agents within are capable of mutation and adaptation.

Metaphoria possesses a great number of stochastic processes and user control over many different parameters. The complexity of Metaphoria would require years to examine all possible aspects of this model regarding money distribution. Regardless, it was thought that the initial finding was interesting enough to report. The simulation at settings the simulator was left in from the last testing revealed a stationary distribution of money measured at 0.5 Gini coefficient (Fig. 8.7).

In subsequent testing, it was easy to find configurations where the Gini coefficient of money moved slightly below 0.5 and above 0.5. It is worth noting that there is tenuous evidence in the experiments suggesting that a 0.5 Gini coefficient of money is important to the dynamics and stability of the system. This is something for future investigation.

8.3 TOY TRADER RATIONALE AND DEFINITIONS

Circular economy is a term introduced to students in most undergraduate economics textbooks. The money flows from consumers to businesses and back to the consumers, because consumers are also the workers who produce the goods that they then consumed. In aggregate, people are given wages for making products that they then turn around and purchase from businesses that employed them. Put succinctly, looked at from the outside, a trade economy is population buying and selling from themselves.

As a worker, the agent's job in the Toy Trader is to sell Toys. Pay is dependent on performance. As a consumer, they desire to purchase 1 Toy per turn. It is a circular economy. While neoclassical models usually reduce the economy to one or two representative consumers, the Toy Trader uses 400 representative worker-consumers buying and selling 2000 of one type of representative goods.

The Toy Trader features no consumption or production. If consumption exceeds production in the long run, products disappear and trade stops. If production exceeds consumption in the long run, the goods supply grows indefinitely and forms a glut. Trade stops.

As common sense dictates, in the long run, overall demand must equal overall production or trade stops. With this in mind, let us set each agent to consume 1 toy per turn. For a long-run trade to exist, this must be balanced by production. Accordingly, we set each agent to produce 1 toy per turn. So, an agent starts with 3 toys in inventory. As a consumer, the agent consumes 1 toy, leaving 2 toys in inventory. Then, as a worker, the same agent produces one toy, leaving 3 toys in inventory. Inventory is back where we started.

In the Toy Trader, production and consumption can be whatever the user imagines it to be.

What if one agent produces all the toys while the others are wage earners and consumers? In this case, the one agent-producer (or the few) will become phenomenally rich. According to the theory of market competition, this triggers new producers to set up shop. In the Toy model, competition is so perfect that everyone has set up shop.

What does money represent in the Toy Trader? In terms of debate and empirical study, money can mean many things (e.g. Friedman & Schwartz, 1969; Graziani, 1996; Kaufman, 1969). When gathering empirical data, it is essential to understand exactly what is being measured to know what data are included. Similarly, models attempting to make real empirical predictions must have clear definitions of the money it is claiming to represent in order to match the results to empirical data. Failures in definition can skew the results and create mismatches between predictive models and reality.

On the other hand, Toy Trader is designed to further understandings of the trade forces emerging from a basic trade system regardless of the kind of liquid money. Toy Trader money could represent cigarettes used by prisoners or fiat money that dominates modern economies. Accordingly, money in the Toy Trader model is that which exists and is accepted for the purposes of trade, regardless of how that money was created and came to be the accepted currency. As the Toy Trader model money is immediately available for trade, it would best be equated to M0 or M1 in a modern economy. Other than this, there is nothing that defines the money in the Toy Trader model as having the qualities related to fiat money or not, intrinsically valuable money or not, legal money or not.

Similarly, the Toy Trader model does not start with a definition for its agents. Generally, the Toy Trader model agents represent any entity with the power to buy and/or sell. They could represent consumers, businesses, countries, or perhaps teenagers between the ages of 14 and 17.

Finally, the goods are that which is sold or purchased in exchange for money. They are called 'Toys' in the Toy Trader model purely for convenience, but they can represent anything traded, including services. Despite the model's name, this work is not meant to be a specialised interrogation of toy market trade dynamics.

The Toy Trader model distils trade to its most basic level, allowing us to examine the naked results. Adding intermediate steps may or may not significantly influence the overall systemic shapes arising from trade. However, no matter how many complications are layered on top of the basic dynamics of trade, the core forces revealed by the Toy Trader will remain. Anyone seeking to build a fair society underneath a trade economy needs to be aware of the foundational forces arising from trade.

8.4   THE GINI COEFFICIENT

It is important to note that the Gini coefficient is only one possible measure of inequality and is not necessarily objectively accurate. For example, the Gini coefficient is said to range from 0 (perfect equality) to 1 (perfect inequality). However, in agent-based model experiments that feature debt, it is possible to see a measured Gini coefficient of greater than one.

The data necessary to measure inequality are much harder to obtain in the real world than it is in a simulation. Many people are loath to divulge accurate income or wealth data. One of the easiest data sets to come by in modern countries is income distribution as reported by taxes. Yet, some might note that not everyone is absolutely honest about their taxes.

Milanovic (2012) suggests that there are at least three meaningful ways of calculating the Gini coefficient in the world. Concept 1 treats the income of countries as single individuals and measures the world inequality accordingly. Concept 2 weighs each country's income according to their population and measures the inequality from the results. Concept 3 attempts to measure individual income throughout the world regardless of their country of origin. These all yield different Gini coefficients. Regardless, the Gini coefficient can be used effectively as a relative measure and a measure of trends.

If we measure the Gini coefficient of the incomes of several countries and compare it to the world using concept 3, we discover that the world exhibits the highest inequality at 0.7, while the US, it is around 0.4 and Sweden is approximately 0.26 (Milanovic, 2012, p. 9). On the other hand, if we use concept 1 and map the Gini index of the world, between 1960 and 2010, the Gini fluctuates between 0.46 and 0.55 (Milanovic, 2005, pp. 180–181).

The subject of the Gini coefficient and other measures of inequality can and do take up entire books. This is only a brief overview of the topic as the Gini coefficient is prominent in this work.

Regardless, no one measures the Gini coefficient of money alone as is done in these simulations. As such, it is impossible to validate the 0.5 money distribution Gini coefficient using real data. The closest empirical data are the Gini coefficient of income distribution. Even if we could measure individual holdings of money as we do in the simulation, just as with the Gini coefficient, the final result would largely depend on how money is defined.

Furthermore, as will be explored in Chapter 12, it is possible to configure the Toy Trader, so the Gini coefficient of money stabilises much higher than 0.5.

8.5   SUMMARY

In summary, two points of interest come from these experiments. One is that econophysicists are right about the money stabilising in a Boltzmann–Gibbs distribution in certain conditions. However, even experiments done with a simulation as simple the Toy Trader model suggest that this topic is more complicated than the Dragulescu and Yakovenko (2000) paper suggests. In fact, these experimental results are supportive of criticisms made by Gallegati et al. (2006) where they challenge econophysicists about too quickly attempting to fit statistical distributions to empirical data. Overall, the money distribution does tend to go to 0.5 Gini coefficient in an efficient economy, but there are several factors even in a very simple trade model that can move the Gini away from 0.5.

The second point is that in a closed trade system where there is a fixed amount of money, barter is not the result. Money tends to distribute itself to a 0.5 Gini distribution more readily than do other measures of wealth. In other words, money behaves uniquely among commodities, even if the supply of both is fixed.

Thinking in dynamic terms, money has an active agency while any good or service is passive. The person with the most commodities cannot force another agent to buy from their stock (e.g. others are selling at a lower price, better location, etc.). A commodity-rich agent must wait for someone with money to agree to purchase at their asking price. On the other hand, the person with the most money can outbid anyone and buy a commodity at any time there is a supply being offered. In a nutshell, money represents power in a market system in a way that nothing else does, regardless of whether money supply is fixed or fiat.

It is worth noting that there is a hint in the experiments that a 0.5 Gini coefficient of money may be significant to the stability of trading systems. Where the Gini coefficient gets moved away from 0.5, the trade systems tend to exhibit increasing frequencies of endogenous price shocks. However, more work is required before a definitive statement can be made.

These experimental results are not an argument that 0.5 is the empirical Gini distribution of money. What these experiments suggest is that a 0.5 Gini coefficient of money distribution is the starting point of a market system assuming people with equal skill and ability. Bluntly, while poverty can be caused by poor habits, poor habits are not necessity. Without intervention, a poor class will develop through no fault of their own. Equally, a rich class will also develop through no fault of their own. This is important to understand if we are to develop a fair society.

REFERENCES

Boltzmann, L. (1965). Lectures on gas theory. *American Journal of Physics, 33*(11), 974–975.

Davies, J. B., & Shorrocks, A. F. (2000). The distribution of wealth. *Handbook of income distribution, 1*, 605–675.

Dragulescu, A., & Yakovenko, V. M. (2000). Statistical mechanics of money. *The European Physical Journal B-Condensed Matter and Complex Systems, 17*(4), 723–729.

Friedman, M., & Schwartz, A. J. (1969). The definition of money: Net wealth and neutrality as criteria. *Journal of Money, Credit and Banking, 1*(1), 1–14.

Gallegati, M., Keen, S., Lux, T., & Ormerod, P. (2006). Worrying trends in econophysics. *Physica A: Statistical Mechanics and its Applications, 370*(1), 1–6.

Galor, O., & Zeira, J. (1993). Income distribution and macroeconomics. *The Review of Economic Studies, 60*(1), 35–52.

Graziani, A. (1996). Money as purchasing power and money as a stock of wealth in Keynesian economic thought. In G. Deleplace & E. J. Nell (Eds.), *Money in motion* (pp. 139–154). Houndmills, Basingstoke and London, UK: Palgrave Macmillan.

Kaufman, G. G. (1969). More on an empirical definition of money. *The American Economic Review, 59*(1), 78–87.

Keister, L. A. (2000). *Wealth in America: Trends in wealth inequality.* Cambridge: Cambridge University Press.

Kohler, T. A., Smith, M. E., Bogaard, A., Feinman, G. M., Peterson, C. E., Betzenhauser, A., ... & Ellyson, L. J. (2017). Greater post-Neolithic wealth disparities in Eurasia than in North America and Mesoamerica. *Nature*, nature24646.

Kuznets, S. (1955). Economic growth and income inequality. *The American Economic Review, 45*(1), 1–28.

Milanovic, B. (2005). *Worlds Apart: Measuring global and international inequality*. Retrieved March 8, 2011, from http://siteresources.worldbank.org/INTPOVRES/Resources/477227-1142020443961/Module5_chap9_10.pdf.

Milanovic, B. (2012). *Global income inequality by the numbers: In history and now—An overview* (Policy Research Working Paper 6259). The World Bank Development Research.

Piketty, T. (2015). About. *American Economic Review, 105*(5), 48–53. https://doi.org/10.1257/aer.p20151060.

Wannier, G. H. (1987). *Statistical physics*. New York: Dover.

Wilensky, U., & Rand, W. (2015). *An introduction to agent-based modeling: Modeling natural, social, and engineered complex systems with Netlogo*. Cambridge: MIT Press.

Yakovenko, V. M. (2016). Monetary economics from econophysics perspective. *arXiv preprint arXiv:1608.04832*.

CHAPTER 9

System Efficiency

Abstract It is frequently said that the market economy is the most efficient economic organisation ever devised by human kind. However, numerous complexity experiments indicate that agent computational effort is inversely correlated with system efficiency. The market economy puts consider computation pressure on consumers because of the wide range of choice and prices available in a market economy. The Toy Trader model is used to test whether normal complexity characteristics hold true in monetary trade systems.

Keywords Efficiency · Perfect information · Computational power · El Farol · Tit for Tat · Prisoner's dilemma · Evolution · Agent-based model · Netlogo · Toy Trader model

What do we know about trade efficiency in a complex system? According to linear-system models, more agent knowledge leads to more market efficiency. Conveniently, an agent with perfect information also makes linear-system models easier to solve. In more advanced work, there have been attempts to incorporate imperfect information (e.g. Collard, Dellas, & Smets, 2009; De Grauwe, 2008; Lorenzoni, 2005). Post-Keynesians also theorise about the economy in the presence of asymmetric or uncertain information (e.g. Dymski, 1993; Fontana & Gerrard, 2004; Van Ees & Garretsen, 1993).

© The Author(s) 2019
T. Gooding, *Economics for a Fairer Society*,
https://doi.org/10.1007/978-3-030-17020-2_9

In complex systems, the situation is reversed: more agent computation leads to less efficiency. In real-world terms, more consumer choice will lead to a less efficient economy, because more choice means more computation effort by the consumer. It follows that a system populated by omniscient rational agents would lead to the least efficient market possible in this regard.

9.1   Defining Efficiency

A key argument arising from linear-system theory is that well-managed free markets drive towards Pareto efficiency. A Pareto efficient market is one where no person can be made better off without making someone else worse off (were this ever realised, trade would stop). In this context, efficiency is measured against an 'optimal' distribution and utilisation of scarce resources. The key free-market mechanism that guides markets towards Pareto efficiency is price.

According to linear-system models, price is causally linked to supply and demand and therefore indicates shortages and surpluses. Price swings intrinsically motivate people to selfishly respond in an economic manner that benefits all in society. For example, if there is a water shortage due to a disaster, the price of water will go up. This will create profit opportunities which will bring in new entrepreneurs seeking profit. Their activity will increase the water supply, and thus the water shortage will be solved to the best of the system's ability. Businesses are happy because they are making profits and consumers are happy because water is now available through the mechanisms of the free-market system.

However, sometimes it takes time for the prices to move. Prices that 'stick' to old levels are called 'sticky prices'. Sticky prices are a problem because whenever they get stuck at levels away from the linear-system equilibrium price, prices are not accurately promoting efficient distributions. Therefore, a key indicator of economic efficiency is the speed at which price moves.

Another way prices can become incorrect is through price oscillation. Whenever a price oscillates away from the 'correct' price, price is failing to indicate the most efficient resource distribution. Accordingly, the lack of price oscillations correlates to greater economic efficiency.

In a trade system, the only way resources can be distributed is through trade. Therefore, a portion of the population being forced out of trade, and therefore removed from the distribution system, indicates the presence of serious trade inefficiencies. Therefore, the proportion of the population that is able to trade is correlates with economic efficiency.

These three measures of efficiency—speed of price movement, (lack of) oscillations, and trade participation—are used as indicators of economic efficiency in the following experiments.

9.2   EL FAROL

El Farol is a famous economic complexity problem posed by Arthur (1994). A consumer wants to go to a popular bar with live singing, but only if it is not too crowded. If it is too crowded, it is unpleasant and therefore a waste of time and money. There are no means for the consumer to determine in advance whether it will be crowded or not. For a consumer to make a rational decision, the consumer must successfully predict what other equally rational consumers are going to do. As the price is always the same, there is no unique price information available to form a signal. What is a rational consumer to do?

If all agents have perfect information they all have the same information. It follows that a population of rational agents will always make the same decision. This homogeneous response will create a binary outcome: either everyone will go to the bar, leading to overcrowding, or no one will go. The success rate of a system populated by classical rational agents is 0%. In fact, any model assuming homogeneous agents making the same decision necessarily fails. The only possible way to successfully model this problem is to assume heterogeneous agents acting on imperfect information. Note that heterogenous agents with perfect information leads to an unresolvable feedback; agent 1 knows that agent 2 knows that agent 1 knows that agent 2 knows … ad infinitum.

Arthur set up an evolutionary agent-based model whereby the agents had a set number of pre-designed strategies from which to choose. They implemented strategies according to its past success. The result was a better than average success rate. In his 1994 paper, Arthur suggests that a pure evolutionary algorithm, such as a genetic algorithm, would likely do no better.

9.3   THE RAND/STONEDAHL HYPOTHESIS

Arthur's suggestion led to Rand and Stonedahl (2007) to run some experiments in the El Farol environment to compare the performance of Arthur's bundle of strategies with a pure evolutionary algorithm. Their experiments had a surprising outcome: the more computational effort they gave their agents, the less efficient the system became.

One indication of the inefficiency was the appearance of chaotic oscillations in the simulation. Specifically, '… allowing the agents more time to evolve their strategies results in a greater amplitude of the chaotic oscillation in attendance. […] However, precisely why additional computational resources cause an increase in the size of the fluctuations remains a subject for further study' (ibid., p. 80).

This result is eluded to in earlier work done by Hogg and Huberman (1991) where they demonstrated that in an agent-based model, simple instruction can reach a similar level of efficiency as an omniscient and omnipotent presence governing the system. Furthermore, several other experiments support the conclusion that additional computation at the agent level can impede efficiency.

Consider the two prisoner's dilemma tournaments held by Axelrod and Hamilton (1981) in 1980. This was a tournament where individual programs would repeatedly interact with one another under rules of the prisoner's dilemma. Axelrod and Hamilton sent open invitations to programmers all over the world to compete. Many programs were received, some of which were quite sophisticated. For example, one program modelled the behaviour of other players as a Markov process and then used Bayesian inference to select what seemed the best choice for the long run. Regardless, the winner was Tit for Tat, the simplest program submitted to the tournament. The winner and its strategy were announced, and the tournament offered again. Tit for Tat won again.

Low computation won again in 1990 when a double-auction tournament was held by the Santa Fe Institute. Programmers were invited to compete within an artificial trade market (Rust, Miller, & Palmer, 1994). Thirty programs were received, some of which contained sophisticated learning algorithms involving the ideas from artificial intelligence and cognitive science. The tournament winner was again one of the simplest programs submitted.

In another experiment, Wilhite (2001) tested the efficiency of trade networks in terms of maximising 'utility' in a bilateral trading environment involving two products; 500 agents were initiated with a random bundle of goods with varying 'utility'. They then used trade to increase the utility of their bundle of goods. Wilhite tested four types of networks.

1. All traders could trade with all other traders.
2. Traders were locked into 10 isolated groups of 50 each.

3. The same as group 2 except the two end agents were members of both their own trading group and that of the neighbouring group (creating two links).
4. The same as group 3 except some groups had a single additional link to another random distant group.

For the purpose of this work, we note that the 'small world network' not only created the best outcome, but it did it with the fewest searches. In other words, it was computationally the least intensive while being the most efficient. It is also interesting that while it was computationally efficient, this system averaged the most trades of all the networks. The trade system with 'perfect information', where all agents can see and trade with all other agents, was considerably less efficient in terms of ultimate utility while being the most computationally intensive.

The final example is a fascinating result that appeared in a prisoner's dilemma scenario that was set up using agents with considerable computational resources, including 'a simple language to think with and enough resources to have memories and to act on them' (Dedeo, 2017, paragraph 6). The two experimenters, Dedeo and Miller, were expecting a Tit-for-Tat strategy to become dominant as had happened in so many other prisoner dilemma experiments, but this was not the case. The eventual dominating agents were characterised as having 'a taste for genocide' (Dedeo, 2017, paragraph 1).

In their experiments, once a dominant culture was established, there was a relative period of peace. The agents dominating the peaceful society had evolved to look for sequences of behaviour that indicated whether other agents were 'one of them'.

Any deviation from the expected sequence was rewarded with total and permanent war. Such a response might take both machines down, in a kind of a digital suicide attack. Because the sequence was so hard to hit upon by accident, only the descendants of ruling machines could profit from the post-code era of selfless cooperation. All others were killed off, including those using the tit-for-tat strategy. This domination would last until enough errors accumulated in the code handed down between generations for dominant machines to stop recognizing each other. Then, they would turn against each other as viciously as they once turned against outsiders, in a kind of population-level autoimmune disease. (Dedeo, 2017, paragraph 11)

While this experiment is interesting on many levels, it demonstrates how increasing the agents' cognitive resources (compared to the simpler programs in the earlier prisoner's dilemma competitions) results in a less stable system. In terms of efficiency, this environment fails because a proportion of the population is prevented from trading due to genocide.

9.4   TOY TRADER EFFICIENCY

The following experiments test the Rand/Stonedahl hypothesis using the Toy Trader model (described in Sect. 8.2). The tool used to control efficiency in the Toy Trader model is a slider in the model called market-sight that adjusts the radius of the agents' price and goods detection. The higher market-sight, the greater the distance the agents can see and the greater the computational resources required by each agent. When market-sight is set to its maximum of 25, the simulation runs relatively slowly, physically demonstrating the increased computational intensity. On my computer, a Toy Trader simulation with market-sight = 25 took 4 minutes 29 seconds to complete 6000 iterations. When market-sight = 1, ceteris paribus, a 6000-iteration run takes 10 seconds.

As previously mentioned, efficiency is measured in three ways. The first measure comes from the Rand/Stonedahl paper where they note that in their less efficient simulation runs, oscillations appear in the result. The second measure is the speed in iterations that it takes for the price to stabilise in each model configuration. The third is the degree to which the population can continue trading.

To aid in the demonstration, the Gini Coefficient graphs are joined to two new graphs: Number of Trades and Wealth by Percentage. Unless otherwise stated, wealth has been set to money only in the wealth distribution graphs.

First, we look for the oscillations that were evident in the Rand/Stonedahl experiments. As noted in Chapter 5, Netlogo graphs automatically compress hiding much of the detail. To check for oscillations, runs to 600 iterations were made in the two market-sight configurations.

Graphs

- **Number of Trades**—Sums the number of trades that take place during each iteration.

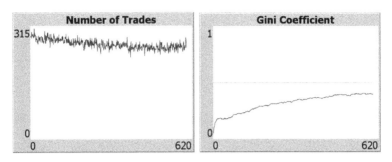

Fig. 9.1   Market-sight 1, 600 iterations

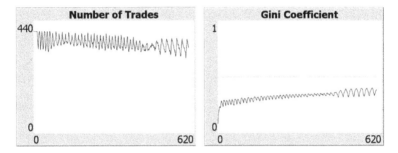

Fig. 9.2   Market-sight 25, 600 iterations

The first run is the most efficient according to the Rand/Stonedahl hypothesis. There is noise evident in the Number of Trades graph, but there are no oscillations evident (Fig. 9.1).

Figure 9.2 shows a simulation run with Market-sight set to 25. This greatly increases the computation load on the agents.

As with Rand/Stonedalh's work, oscillations appear. Furthermore, if this configuration is run indefinitely, trade collapses usually around the 100,000-iteration mark. On the other hand, a Toy Trader run using market-sight = 1 can be run indefinitely with no reduction in trade.

Another way to test the Rand-Stonedahl hypothesis in Toy Trader is to force the agents to use more computational power through circumstance. Significantly increasing population within the same physical space will force agents to use more computational power comparing prices because there will be, on average, more agents within a certain physical space than in previous runs. Figure 9.3 is an identical run to

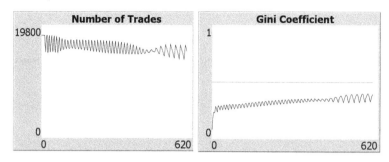

Fig. 9.3   Market-sight 1, population 18,000, 600 iterations

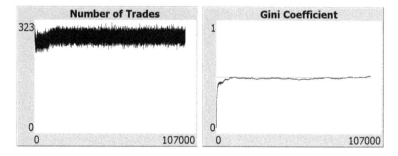

Fig. 9.4   Market-sight 1, 100,000 iterations

Fig. 9.1 (Market-sight = 1) except the population has been increased from 400 to 18,000. Compare to graphs in Fig. 9.2 (population = 400, market-sight = 25).

The second measure of efficiency is the speed at which the simulation run stabilises. In high computational simulation runs (market-sight = 25 or the population = 18,000), it takes many iterations for the system to stabilise. When market-sight = 25, eventually there is a complete trade breakdown. By contrast, a run with market-sight = 1 stabilises in all respects by around 10,000 iterations (Fig. 9.4).

Finally, the third efficiency measure is the degree to which trade is maintained in the trading system. As already has been mentioned, when Market-sight is set to 25, trade tends to stop completely. On the other hand, when Market-sight is set to 1, trade stabilises at a relatively high level as can be seen in the Number of Trades chart in Fig. 9.4 which is run to 100,000 iterations. Compare to Fig. 9.5 (market-sight = 25, population = 400). Note that the flat lines at the very end indicate no trades.

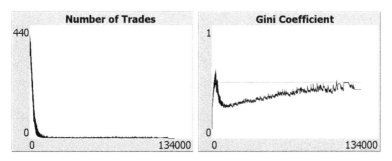

Fig. 9.5   Market-sight 25, 120,000 iterations

9.5   Summary

Evidence produced by the Toy Trader model is consistent with other complexity experiment outcomes indicating that agent computational power is inversely proportional to overall system efficiency. In the absence of evolutionary forces, whenever agent computational effort is increased the Toy Trader model tends to exhibit rising prices while an increasing portion of the population is forced out of trade. This suggests that models that assume perfect information represent the least efficient trading system possible. It also suggests that creating more consumer choice and the increasing population density could be making our trading systems less efficient as more choice requires more computational effort from the consumer.

This premise appears to be contradicted by empirical productivity figures (Rauch, 1993). It is true that too few agents in an area results in less efficient trading in a given time period, as fewer trades will take place. However, once maximum efficiency is reached, this work implies that increasing the population density further will create systemic economic inefficiencies due to greater choice.

It is also worth noting that most real-world efficiency calculations use price as the root measurement. Price is also at the foundational of most empirical economic data collected today. This is done on the premise that price is a sound indication of value and of the market fundamentals of supply and demand. The next chapter examines the key economic premise that price is a reliable indicator of supply and demand, and therefore, value.

Finally, it would be remiss to invoke computational power without mentioning energy. As biologists have long recognised, computation requires energy and energy requirements are key to the shape of systems (Brooks et al., 1983). This includes the generation, transmission, and the storage of computer programmes that at least some economists see as 'free', as was the loose consensus at the 2017 Edinburgh INET conference held 22 February. However, no construct, whether physical or informational, can be made without energy. For example, the internet currently consumes approximately 70 billion kilowatt-hours per year (Helman, 2016). Energy is the most unforgiving physical constraint of any system. While this work concentrates on the most basic outcomes of trade, a future hope is to build a basic thermodynamic model of the market.

REFERENCES

Arthur, W. (1994). Inductive reasoning and bounded rationality. *The American Economic Review, 84*(2), 406–411.

Axelrod, R., & Hamilton, W. D. (1981, March 27). The evolution of cooperation. *Science, 211*(4489), 1390–1396.

Brooks, B. R., Bruccoleri, R. E., Olafson, B. D., States, D. J., Swaminathan, S. A., & Karplus, M. (1983). CHARMM: A program for macromolecular energy, minimization, and dynamics calculations. *Journal of Computational Chemistry, 4*(2), 187–217.

Collard, F., Dellas, H., & Smets, F. (2009). Imperfect information and the business cycle. *Journal of Monetary Economics, 56*, S38–S56.

Dedeo, S. (2017, September 17). Is tribalism a nature malfunction? What computers teach us about getting along. *Nautalus*. Retrieved from http://nautil.us/issue/52/the-hive/is-tribalism a natural-malfunction.

De Grauwe, P. (2008). *DSGE-modelling: When agents are imperfectly informed* (European Central Bank Working Paper No. 897).

Dymski, G. A. (1993). Keynesian uncertainty and asymmetric information: Complementary or contradictory? *Journal of Post Keynesian Economics, 16*(1), 49–54.

Fontana, G., & Gerrard, B. (2004). A post Keynesian theory of decision making under uncertainty. *Journal of Economic Psychology, 25*(5), 619–637.

Helman, C. (2016, June 28). *Berkeley lab: It takes 70 billion kilowatt hours a year to run the internet*. Retrieved October 28, 2017, from https://www.forbes.com/sites/christopherhelman/2016/06/28/how-much-electricity-does-it-take-to-run-the-internet/.

Hogg, T., & Huberman, B. A. (1991). Controlling chaos in distributed systems. *IEEE Transactions on Systems, Man, and Cybernetics, 21*(6), 1325–1332.

Rauch, J. E. (1993). Productivity gains from geographic concentration of human capital: Evidence from the cities. *Journal of Urban Economics, 34*(3): 380–400.

Lorenzoni, G. (2005). *Imperfect information, consumers' expectations and business cycles*. Cambridge: MIT Mimeo.

Rand, W., & Stonedahl, F. (2007). *The El Farol bar problem and computational effort: Why people fail to use bars efficiently*. Evanston, IL: Northwestern University Press.

Rust, J., Miller, J. H., & Palmer, R. (1994). Characterizing effective trading strategies: Insights from a computerized double auction tournament. *Journal of Economic Dynamics and Control, 18*, 61–96.

Van Ees, H., & Garretsen, H. (1993). Financial markets and the complementarity of asymmetric information and fundamental uncertainty. *Journal of Post Keynesian Economics, 16*(1), 37–48.

Wilhite, A. (2001). Bilateral trade and 'small-world' networks. *Computational Economics, 18*(1), 49–64.

CHAPTER 10

Price Basics

Abstract It is often said that price is determined by supply and demand. Empirical evidence suggests that this is true in the short run. In the long run, time allows for complexity dynamics to become dominant. This chapter examines the behaviour of price in a complex system. Specifically, empirical evolutionary prerequisites present in the markets are introduced to examine their long-term impact.

Keywords Price, supply and demand · Evolution · Mutation · Inequality · Evolutionary prerequisites · Agent-based model · Netlogo · Toy Trader model

What determines long-term price behaviour in a complex system? The nature of price is key to the meritocracy claims made on behalf of a free-market system. Price determines resource allocation and the rewards for different efforts. The dominant societal narrative about the market suggests that if you are rich or poor, it is because you deserve to be, because the free market has made it so.

Anyone following trade markets or who manages a business knows that changes in supply or demand impact prices. Linear-system models accurately capture these dynamics. Even complicating factors are said to act through supply and demand. This research does not dispute this fact. What this chapter explores is the emergent behaviour of price in the

© The Author(s) 2019   89
T. Gooding, *Economics for a Fairer Society*,
https://doi.org/10.1007/978-3-030-17020-2_10

simplest trading system possible. The goal is to understand the basics of long-term prices arising from trade in a complex system.

Current price theories suggest that prices move towards intrinsic values (e.g. Marx's labour theory of value, Kalecki's production cost+mark-up) or towards a price equilibrium derived from supply and demand. Regardless of the starting point, all theories rest on the assumption that supply and demand are the fundamentals that drive price and profits towards predictable stable levels. The price mechanism assumption is a key in assuming that the free market is efficient.

> There exists therefore, in the circumstances which I have described, a tendency towards equilibrium, a tendency, that is, for competition to bring profits towards a uniform level, with, of course, a wide dispersion about the mean. That this is a central feature of free enterprise, and is crucial to the allocative efficiency of the system, that has long been recognized. (Dow & Hillard, 2002, p. 23)

We now test whether these assumptions hold up in a complex system.

10.1   Homogeneous System

This work is not the first to suggest that supply and demand may not determine price. The mainstream economist Gorman (1953) used mathematical proofs to demonstrate that the aggregate demand cannot be said to correlate to price unless all consumers have identical preferences and possess the same spending power. As we know, consumers actually do differ. Ceteris paribus, wherever demand does not correlate to price, supply and demand cannot be said to correlate to price. That makes Gorman one of the first economists to (inadvertently) suggest that price may not be a function of supply and demand.

The physicist Osborne (1977) was much more direct when he stated that supply and demand are insufficient information with which to determine price. Time and space are two of the key physical factors lacking in economic models, Osborne claimed.

In the Toy Trader model, each agent starts with 100 money and 5 toys. With 400 agents, 40,000 money (100 money $\times$ 400 agents) are chasing 2000 toys (5 toys $\times$ 400 agents). Purely for reference, the price of 20 (40,000 money/2000 toys) is marked by a horizontal line on the price charts. The minimum price possible in these experiments is currently set at 0.5 in the model, and thus preventing prices from going to 0. All agents are homogeneous and all agents begin with the same selling price of 10.

Demand can be complicated to define. Is it a measure of those who want to purchase a product, even if they cannot afford to do so, or is it simply a measure of the money being brought to bear by those who can? The second definition means that those who run out of money do not have a demand for anything, including food. This definition might be the correct definition for some, but it lacks humanity. Therefore, we are using the first definition in this work. Even so, as Toys cost 10 each and agents start with 100 money, they all can afford to buy Toys.

During each iteration, every agent attempts to purchase a single toy from another agent at the lowest price it can find. System demand is fixed at 400 toys per iteration. System supply is fixed at 2000 toys per iteration. Supply and demand are fixed in oversupply.

The full Toy Trader model description is available in Sect. 8.2.

Here is the next thought experiment for any trained economist: what do you think the equilibrium price outcome will be after 6000 iterations? As demonstrated in Chapter 6, these non-evolutionary patterns remain stable between runs with only small variations.

Graphs

- **Average Price**—Sums the price of all trades and divides by the number of trades that take place during each iteration. There is a horizontal reference line set at 20 (money supply/total toys at Toy Trader default settings) in most Toy Trader graphs.

Initially, the simulation is set according to the verbal description in Sect. 8.2 (market-sight = 1), meaning that agents have to be within a 1 patch radius in order to trade. This is the most efficient setting possible in the Toy Trader. Recall that the agents are moving in a random direction a distance equal to 1 patch during each iteration. As a result, no agent is permanently left without a trading partner.

As many would expect, with the market in oversupply, the price is driven downwards (Fig. 10.1). Quantitatively, final average price in this particular simulation run is 1.6, though this will vary slightly from run to run. However, wealth is not equally distributed even though the agents have identical ability and opportunity. In this configuration, the Gini coefficient is 0.5 (see Fig. 8.6). In this efficient simple configuration, the Toy Trader model acts much as linear-system theory predicts. A shortage

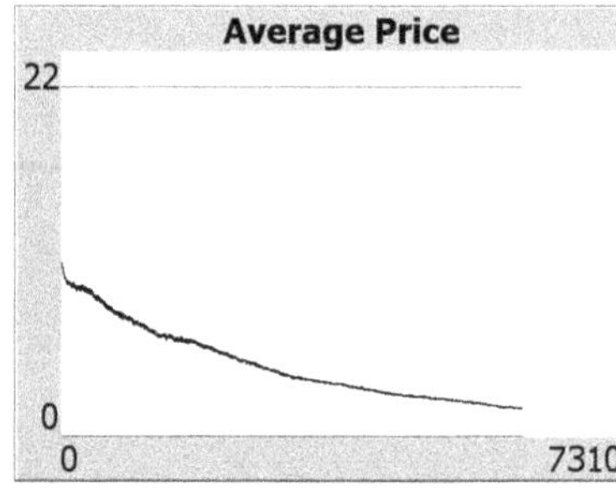

Fig. 10.1   Price, market-sight 1, final price 1.6

Fig. 10.2   Price, market-sight 25, final price 148.4

causes price to rise and if demand and supply are equated a short-term price stability becomes evident.

What if we honour the perfect information assumption, or rational agent, used in most linear-system models? Figure 10.2 shows the resulting price trends when market-sight = 25, meaning all agents know all prices and can trade with any agent in the system, and the system is still in surplus. At no time does the price go down. Quantitatively, final average price in this particular simulation run is 148.

Note that had the simulation been initiated at its final price (148), as all agents start with 100 money, not a single agent would have been able to make a trade. The system first had to redistribute money so that some agents possessed a higher share of money before trade at the higher price is possible. This necessarily pushes poorer agents out of the trading economy. Note that all agents are homogeneous, so this is not the result of a meritocratic process. Instead, look to the core distributional forces in a monetary economy that are examined in Chapter 8. If simulation is run indefinitely in this configuration (perfect information), increasing inequality eventually causes a complete trade breakdown.

A key difference between the Toy Trader model and a linear-system model is that the agents are trading one at a time. As each agent trades, it slightly changes the environment for those who follow. An agent that sold one Toy checks its inventory for a possible price change. This constant change and feedback from the environment make emergent behaviour difficult to mentally grasp. In economics, this idea is partially expressed by the Lucas critique (Lucas, 1976), though the Lucas critique generally includes only a single environmental change and the resulting agent adaptation, rather than cycles of feedback as described by stigmergy. As Wolfram (2002) demonstrated, the feedback cycles in the simplest iterative systems can be impossible anticipate.

In the next experiment, market-sight is set to 2 (Fig. 10.3). In this experiment, agents are required to be within 2 patches of another agent in order to see price and to trade. Note the price still rises, but not as far as it did at when agents had perfect trading information.

The key result of the previous three experiments is that even though we got very different price results, the supply and demand never changed. This occurred even in the simplest trading simulation possible.

One objection to these experiments might be that the results depend on the agents following unrealistically rigid pricing strategies. It is true that the ad hoc pricing algorithms used in Toy Trader do significantly impact the results. Even changing the price up from 1.0101 to 1.0100 can change the patterns, though not the overall trends. Many algorithms have been tested and the results remain largely consistent with the finding that supply and demand do not dominate price in a system where emergent behaviour is present.

In reality, the sensitivity to a specific trading algorithm is not very important because in the real world, prices are set heterogeneously using

Fig. 10.3 Price, market-sight 2, final price 39.7

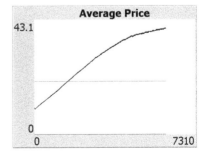

different pricing strategies. Furthermore, these experiments suggest that when agents imitate one another, then evolution dominates the price patterns. This is explored in the next section.

10.2   HETEROGENEOUS PRICING

10.2.1   Introducing Mutation

The first step to creating heterogeneous pricing is to have the homogeneous agents randomly mutate their pricing behaviour. Mutating agents' behaviour is straightforward in an agent-based model. The system is initiated with homogeneous agents just as before. During each iteration, each agent is subjected to the probability of mutating their pricing algorithm. The homogeneous pricing behaviour starts as always:

- price-up: price-new = price-old × 1.0101
- price-down: price-new = price-old × 0.99

At a probability 1 in 5000, the price-up algorithm of a particular agent will be altered in the following manner (in pseudo-code):

- 1.0101 +random 0.01 −random 0.01 → where *random 0.01* randomly chooses a real number between 0 and 0.01 (but not including 0.01).
- If the new number is < 1, set to 1 (prevents 'price up' from becoming 'price down').

This means that 1.0101 will be altered by adding a random number between 0 and 0.01 and then subtracting another random number between 0 and 0.01. This creates an equal chance that the pricing algorithm will be adjusted upwards or downwards. Once the new price algorithm is established, that agent will continue to use it unless and until it is again randomly changed.

Similarly, at probability 1 in 5000, the new price-down algorithm will be altered in the following manner:

- 0.99 +random 0.01 −random 0.01
- if the new number is > 1, set to 1 (prevents 'price down' becoming 'price up')
- if the new number is < 0.001, set to 0.001 (prevents setting prices to 0).

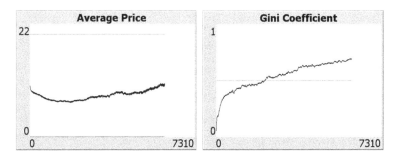

Fig. 10.4   Price and Gini coefficient, mutation probability = 1 in 5000

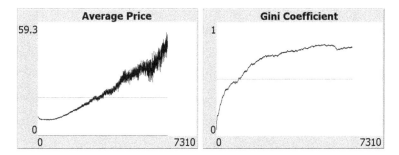

Fig. 10.5   Price and Gini coefficient, mutation probability = 1 in 500

Figure 10.4 shows the price and Gini patterns arising from pricing heterogeneity. These experiments use Market-sight = 1 as it is the most efficient and best fits linear-system predictions (prices normally go down in an oversupplied market).

As the system is initiated with homogeneous agents, the initial trend is identical to the homogeneous run seen in Fig. 10.1 (Market-sight = 1). However, as agent heterogeneity increases, the two systems diverge; prices begin to inflate, and the distribution of money rises above a 0.5 Gini coefficient.

If the mutation rate is increased to a probability of 1 in 500, the effects of heterogeneity become more pronounced (Fig. 10.5). Note the impact on inequality.

This outcome makes intuitive sense. Agents trading with more successful pricing behaviour will go on to accumulate a greater share of wealth, whereas agents with less successful strategies become poorer.

The price increases because fewer agents trading with more money is a practical equivalent to increasing the money supply.

Note that perfect information rules out heterogeneous agents as it implies that everyone has the same information and uses the same best strategy. Furthermore, perfect information constitutes all information from the past, present, and future. If perfect information is infinite, then according to the laws of thermodynamics, infinite energy is required to manage it. The laws of thermodynamics are rarely considered by economists.

10.2.2   Activating the Fitness Test

In the real world, people who find themselves poor relative to other people frequently seek to improve their situation. Many seek to learn the ways that the rich became rich and attempt to imitate them. Things become slightly complicated here as the measure of success is not always the same thing. For example, measuring success in asset markets usually includes the value of their assets. For example, homeowners, investors in blue chip stocks, collectables, etc., count the value of the long-term asset as part of their wealth. Price charts from this type markets tend to exhibit long-run price increases. For example, Fig. 10.6 shows the trading price of the Dow Jones since 1970, the UK housing market since 1975, and the Hang Seng since 1987. Note the persistent asset price inflation.

By contrast, there are markets where traders measure success only by money made. For example, no one puts sugar into a freezer hoping for long-term price rises. The reasoning is sound, as the long-run price in these markets tend to go sideways. In addition, to quote one of my critics, prices tend to flail about wildly. Figure 10.7 shows cotton and coffee since 1972, and Sugar since 1970.

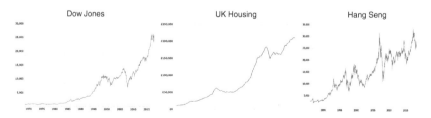

Fig. 10.6   Asset markets: Index charts Macrotrends (n.d.), UK housing figures from Nationwide (n.d.)

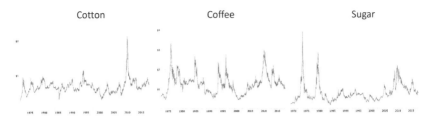

Fig. 10.7   Speculation markets: Macrotrends (n.d.)

Note that the charts from Figs. 10.6 and 10.7 are shown with no inflation adjustment.

In both types of markets, poorer agents attempt to emulate the behaviour of richer agents in the hopes of achieving better success. This is exemplified by the lucrative market of books, talks, websites, television shows, etc., describing the characteristics and habits of the rich and famous people. In some markets, such as the financial markets, trader imitation has been formally studied (e.g. Cont & Bouchaud, 2000).

To define rich and poor in a simulation, the measurement of wealth needs to be explicit. This work focuses in on the evolutionary prerequisites in asset markets and speculation markets. Therefore, the two wealth measures are: (1) money and (2) assets (money + toys × average-price). These two wealth measurements define the two different fitness tests used in these experiments.

Including imitation in the Toy Trader model is simple. First, the definitions of successful and unsuccessful are established. Successful agents are those in the top 5% of all agents when measured by the fitness test. Unsuccessful agents are defined as those in the bottom 50%. This creates a moderate strength evolutionary force. If the bottom 95% were all imitating the successful at these settings (there other ways to moderate the evolutionary force), the evolutionary force becomes too strong to replicate empirical patterns.

For those who would prefer a verbal justification for this set-up, the agents who have wealth measured between 50 and 95% can be considered middle-class and therefore not poor enough to worry excessively about becoming more successful and yet not rich enough to be considered 'celebrities' in their society. Accordingly, they do not feel the need to actively change their behaviour, nor do other agents seek to emulate them. Regardless, these percentages are user-adjustable in the Toy Trader model if you wish to experiment.

The first fitness test used is money, meaning the agents are ranked according to how much money they have. Like Reynold's flocking birds, what we are looking for is the price patterns to look like those from Fig. 10.7. Figure 10.8 shows three runs using a fitness test of money, those with the market fitness test characterised by the markets in Fig. 10.7.

Price Strategy Emulation

1. Set price change Mutation probability to 1 in 180 (see Sect. 10.2.1).
2. Ask poor agents—at probability 1 in 10, set price the same as a random rich agent's price.
3. If (1) is true, at probability 1 in 2, copy the rich agent's price-up algorithm and mutate (add a random number between −0.01 and 0.01).
4. If (1) is true, at probability 1 in 2, copy the rich agent's price-down price algorithm and mutate (add a random number between −0.01 and 0.01).

It is important to be clear about implications of these results. There is no claim that evolution is the sole cause of market volatility in speculation markets, nor is there a claim that the supply and demand never impact price. What is being claimed is that the characteristics of speculation markets contain the necessary prerequisites to create an evolutionary system (agent heterogeneity and success imitation). Furthermore, the resulting evolutionary system is sufficient by itself to explain the characteristic price shapes in speculation markets. This research suggests that any

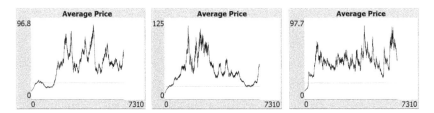

Fig. 10.8   Price, fitness test = money

agent-based model will exhibit the empirically recognisable patterns as long as there is agent imitation and heterogeneity such that the correct evolutionary strength emerges.

The significance of the result becomes more apparent once the fitness test is changed.

In the asset markets, the price of an asset is considered part of the success. For example, home owners frequently consider the price of their house as part of their wealth even if they have no intention of selling and realising the profits. To model these markets, a fitness test of assets (money + toys × average-price) is used. According to research, the price of asset markets tends to trend upwards, regardless of what that asset may be (Okusanya, 2018), just as they do in Fig. 10.6.

Figure 10.9 features the price pattern of the Toy Trader model when the fitness test is changed to assets. Note that in all other respects, the Toy Trader conditions are identical to the runs shown in Fig. 10.8.

Remember, this market is in surplus. Also keep in mind that price is limited by the fixed money supply. Increase the money supply, as is the case in reality, and price would have no upper limit. The robustness of these evolutionary patterns are statistically reflected in Tables 7.5 and 7.6.

Just as with the RobbyGA model, changing the fitness test in the middle of the run creates a stark contrast between the shapes of price under the two different fitness tests (Fig. 10.10). This is a run of 12,000 iterations, divided into four runs of 3000 each. The fitness test was assets, money, assets, and finally, money. The vertical line signifies the exact point the fitness test was changed. Note that the Gini coefficient of money is running close to 0.5 throughout.

Fig. 10.9 Price, fitness test = assets

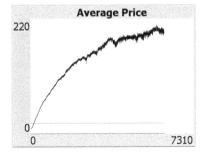

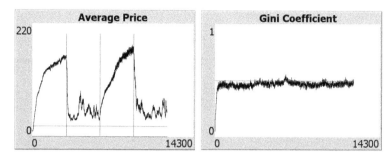

Fig. 10.10   Price and Gini coefficient: Fitness test switched every 3000 iterations

10.3   A Closer Look: UK House Prices

Housing markets have exhibited long-run price rises in many developed economies. For example, the unadjusted UK housing price data between 1952 and 2017 from Nationwide (n.d.) shows an 11,410% actual price rise, and a 352% price rise if it is adjusted for inflation using Bank of England inflation figures. If the supply and demand theory of price is correct, then demand must have significantly outstripped supply. This is what the UK government assumed when it declared: 'In the housing White Paper, "Fixing our broken housing market", we made it clear that our priority is building the new homes this country needs' (Ministry of Housing, Communities and Local Government, 2018).

However, examining the fundamentals underlying this market suggests that the reverse is true—supply has outstripped demand in the long-term. Government figures indicate a 98.8% increase in UK dwellings (DCLG, n.d.) between 1952 and 2017 while the UK population increased only 28.4% between 1951 and 2014 (Office for National Statistics, n.d.), or 31.3% between 1950 and 2018 if we accept a website 'tracking' the UK population in real time (U.K. Population [LIVE], n.d.). Furthermore, recent report (Redfern, 2016) suggests that there is no physical dwelling shortage in any area of the UK, including London and the Southeast. For those interested in more detail, the economist that did the research for the Redfern report has posted details online (Mulheirn, 2017; Mulheirn, n.d.).

10.4   Summary

What the research in this book suggests is that supply and demand might be subservient to evolutionary prerequisites in the long run. If the prerequisites create evolutionary pressures for price increases, prices will go up irrespective of supply and demand.

There is no dispute that supply and demand influence price in the short run. However, to conclude that short-run linear-system dynamics necessarily create long-term equilibria may be without foundation. The experiments suggest that in markets where there is no fitness test, prices can stabilise at an 'equilibrium' such as in Figs. 10.1 and 10.3. However, even non-evolutionary models suggest that it cannot be guaranteed that price is an indication of 'allocative efficiency of the system' (Dow & Hillard, 2002, p. 23). Altering aspects unrelated to aggregate supply and demand, such as the agents' ability to detect prices, significantly impacts the price dynamics.

These experiments also indicate that intrinsic values do not play a large role in determining the long-run price. If one argues that there is no value in the Toy Trader model, then where is the price coming from and why does it look so much like those from reality? If one accepts that the desired inventory in the Toy Trader model successfully captures the agency of value, then why does the equilibrium price disappear as more realistic attributes are added? Of course, the labour theory of value suggests that the price in the Toy Trader model must always go to the minimum, as there is no labour in the model.

This is not to suggest that the price theories developed in various schools of thought have no value at all. In the short time term, ceteris paribus applies as emergent behaviour and evolution do not have time to form. This is perhaps why mainstream theory is successful in the short run but tends to fail in the long run.

Agents setting prices, such as production cost + mark-up (Kalecki, 1944), is valid for individual firms, but this is unlikely to be causal in determining the eventual market price. Any agent autonomously setting a price may or may not sell their wares, as is the case in the Toy Trader model. As such, one cannot say that a price is determined by price setting alone. Only when prices resolve in trade does the price become relevant, as suggested by Friedman (1976) and most mainstream theorists.

Overall, assuming an equilibrium from an economic system with a set amount of supply and demand is an over-simplification. Wealth redistribution, especially as described in Chapter 8, impacts prices. However, the most powerful long-run price influence seems to be evolution. When the fitness test is money alone, the price takes on patterns that are characteristic of those from speculative trading markets, like the financial or commodity markets. When the fitness test combines money and an asset, that market tends to experience price asset inflation, even where there is an excess of supply. This is perhaps best exemplified by modern housing markets.

In accordance with system theory, allowing agents a greater view of prices results in a less efficient trading system. This is perhaps because an individual optimising using their own resources can never match the computational resources available to the system as a whole. This is arguably the understanding that motivates many *laisse-faire* economists and policy-makers. The key problem with this outlook is a misplaced faith in the purity of the price signal.

The next chapter further tests the robustness of this outcome and examines the dynamics of long and short price outcomes in more detail.

REFERENCES

Cont, R., & Bouchaud, J. P. (2000). Herd behavior and aggregate fluctuations in financial markets. *Macroeconomic Dynamics, 4*(2), 170–196.

DCLG. (n.d.). *Live tables on house building: New build dwellings.* Retrieved April 19, 2018, from https://www.gov.uk/government/statistical-data-sets/live-tables-on-house-building.

Dow, S. C., & Hillard, J. (Eds.). (2002). *Keynes, uncertainty and the global economy: Beyond Keynes* (Vol. 2). Cheltenham: Edward Elgar.

Friedman, M. (1976). *Price theory.* New York: Aldine.

Gorman, W. (1953). Community preference fields. *Econometrica, 21*(1), 63–80.

Kalecki, M. (1944). *Studies in economic dynamics.* London: Allen & Unwin.

Lucas, R. E. (1976, January). Econometric policy evaluation: A critique. In K. Brunner & A. H. Meltzer (Eds.), *Carnegie-Rochester conference series on public policy* (Vol. 1, pp. 19–46). Amsterdam: North-Holland.

Macrotrends | The long term perspective on markets. (n.d.). Retrieved February 22, 2019, from https://www.macrotrends.net/.

Ministry of Housing, Communities and Local Government. (2018). *Government response to the housing white paper consultation: Fixing our broken housing market. A summary of consultation responses and the government's view on the way forward*. Retrieved from https://assets.publishing.service.gov.uk/government/uploads/system/uploads/attachment_data/file/685297/Government_response_to_the_housing_White_Paper_consultation.pdf.

Mulheirn, I. (2017, December 18). *How to find a housing shortage… in three misleading charts*. Retrieved April 17, 2018, from https://medium.com/@ian.mulheirn/how-to-find-a-housing-shortage-in-three-misleading-charts-2ee-5ba5d3c38.

Mulheirn, I. (n.d.). *Ian Mulheirn: Medium*. Retrieved August 14, 2018, from https://medium.com/@ian.mulheirn.

Nationwide. (n.d.). Retrieved July 25, 2017, from https://www.nationwide.co.uk/about/house-price-index/download-data#~.

Office for National Statistics. (n.d.). *User requested data: UK population estimates 1851 to 2014*. Retrieved from https://www.ons.gov.uk/peoplepopulationandcommunity/populationandmigration/populationestimates/adhocs/004356ukpopulationestimates1851to2014.

Okusanya, A. (2018, March 28). *Lessons from 118 years of asset class returns data*. Retrieved June 10, 2018, from https://finalytiq.co.uk/lessons-118-years-capital-market-return-data/.

Osborne, M. F. (1977). *Stock market and finance from a physicist's viewpoint*. Minneapolis: Crossgar Press.

Redfern, P. (2016). *The Redfern review into the decline of home ownership*. Retrieved from https://www.redfernreview.org.

U.K. Population (LIVE). (n.d.). Retrieved from http://www.worldometers.info/world-population/uk-population/.

Wolfram, S. (2002). *A new kind of science* (Vol. 5). Champaign: Wolfram Media.

CHAPTER 11

Evolutionary Price Robustness

Abstract Having demonstrated the impact of evolution on price patterns, we test its robustness: the code is changed, products are added, and variables altered. To help explain the results, an old experiment called a double auction is built using Netlogo to demonstrate the difference between short-term and long-term pricing dynamics.

Keywords Price · Supply and demand · Pattern robustness · Pricing algorithms · Evolutionary prerequisites · Evolution · Netlogo · Agent-based models · Toy Trader · Three-Goods Trader · Double-auction model

Are the evolutionary price patterns shown in Chapter 10 merely an artefact of the algorithms built into the Toy Trader? If so, changing the algorithms will change the emerging price patterns. This section examines the robustness of these evolutionary price patterns and offers an insight into why linear-system theory has such a different story than complexity. Specifically, what is causing long-term pricing to deviate from linear-system price theory and short-term empirical observations?

11.1   Pricing Algorithm Changes

Even tiny changes in the price code significantly impact the emergent behaviour of Toy Trader model when mutation and imitation are turned off. However, once the pricing becomes evolutionary, the ad hoc pricing behaviour is no longer dominant, it is evolved. Under evolutionary forces, the results are remarkably robust. This principle is demonstrated by the following experiments where the programmed pricing behaviour is significantly changed.

In the initial experiments, agents blindly alter price according to their stock after each sale. However, if an agent has a high stock and a high selling price but keeps selling products, there is no logical reason for that agent to lower its price. Accordingly, the code is changed to reflect this reality. If an agent makes a sale during an iteration, it no longer lowers its price, even if its stock of toys is very high. This did not change the evolutionary patterns established in Chapter 10.

The pricing algorithms were changed again. This time, the level of stock is removed from all consideration of pricing. This means there are no intrinsic shortages or surpluses. If a sale is made, the agent raises their price. If no sales are made over the course of 2 iterations and the agent has stock, their selling price is lowered.

The reason for the 2-iteration wait before lowering price is that there is a chance that the agent has no available customers during a particular iteration. While it is possible to programme the agents to check for the presence of customers, it would significantly complicate the simulation and raise new modelling questions such as: do we check for customers at the end of the iteration after everyone has moved or include agents that were there but moved away during the iteration? Most computationally intensive would be to check for the presence of customers during all the other agents' turns. While all this new programming is being considered, it is important to keep in mind Chapter 9, System Efficiency.

In its default setting, the traders in the Toy Trader only check their inventory for any price adjustments after a sale, but not after a purchase. There is a setting in the simulation to create 'perfect pricing', pricing where the trader checks their pricing after every purchase and after every sale. Note that this is not really realistic, as real inventory checks are costly and frequently requires business operations to cease until it is completed. Regardless, there were no changes in the overall evolutionary patterns. The prerequisites for a money fitness test created volatile markets while prerequisites for an asset fitness test created asset price inflation.

There is also a setting to turn on 'inventory pricing', which means that the traders do an inventory check after every iteration and make a price adjustment, if necessary, according to their inventory. Again, this made little difference to the resulting price patterns.

The toy trader was also modified so that two other goods were being traded: Crayons and Blackboards. In the Three-Goods Trader model, only Toys was being subjected to a fitness test. The other two products either used the default unevolved code, as described in Sect. 8.2, or used the same price change percentages evolved in the Toy market. In other words, if the standard mark-up for Toys evolved to be 10% for that agent, the mark-up for all products was 10%. There is also a setting that determines whether the traders only imitated the Toy price of the successful trader or whether traders imitated all prices (i.e. toys-price$_{poor}$ = toys-price$_{rich}$; blackboard-price$_{poor}$ = blackboard-price$_{rich}$; crayon-price$_{poor}$ = crayon-price$_{rich}$; subject to the possibility of mutation).

The pricing dynamics of the two new products use the same overall design and algorithms as those used for toys in the original Toy Trader. On the other hand, each product starts with a different stock level and target inventory. At initiation, each agent possesses 5 Toys, 30 Crayons, and 15 Blackboards. The desired stock is 3 for Toys. If the inventory of Toys is 3, the agent will not adjust their selling price. The desired stock for crayons is between 10 and 15 for crayons. If the stock remains between 10 and 15, the price will not change. The desired inventory level for blackboards is between 5 and 8 for blackboards.

The target inventory levels for the new products were chosen randomly and hold no meaning. The range was chosen purely for the purposes of experimentation: I wondered what would happen. These ranges can be moved up and down individually in the simulation if a user wishes to experiment. At the default settings, all products are in surplus in the system.

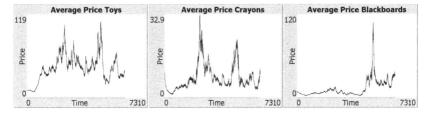

Fig. 11.1   Toys under a money fitness test

This made no difference to the evolutionary patterns. However, if the traders were using the mark-up and mark-down evolved in the Toy market in other markets and poor agents were imitating the prices of all three products, all products took on the same evolutionary shape even though only Toys was being subjected to a fitness test (Fig. 11.1).

11.2   SUPPLY AND DEMAND SHOCKS

These experiments suggest that the impact of supply and demand shocks is more muted in the long run than a linear-system analysis indicates. Instead of price veering to a new level and stabilising in an equilibrium, the price patterns tend to either move or change in volatility when responding to changes in supply and demand.

For example, when the Three-Goods Trader is set so that Toys are subjected to an asset fitness and the desired Toy inventory changed to 7 (Fig. 11.2), the system will be in a shortage condition for one product only, because all agents begin with 5 Toys and desire 7. Note that Fig. 11.2 depicts a run where traders are using price-up = 1.0101 and price-down = 0.99 for Crayons and Blackboards. The evolutionary mark-ups and mark-downs are not being transferred to these two new products.

While the shape of the price chart under evolutionary pressure remains the same, it rises faster and goes to a higher level (with a fixed money supply) than when the Toy inventory is set to 3 (surplus).

If the above configuration is run 100 times with a shortage (desired Toy inventory = 7) and 100 times with a surplus (desire Toy inventory = 3), the descriptive statistics of the final price after 3500 iterations are as follows (Table 11.1).

The effects of a goods shortage on prices shaped by a money fitness test is a bit different. Instead of raising the overall pattern, a shortage

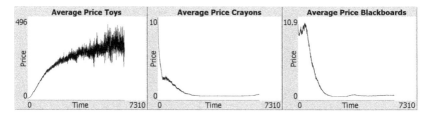

Fig. 11.2   Three-Goods Trader, high demand of toys, asset fitness test

Table 11.1   Statistics of final price of toys ($n = 100$), comparing shortages and surpluses, asset fitness test

Asset fitness test	High demand	Low demand
Mean	282.5	167.1
Maximum	339.0	211.6
Minimum	246.0	135.4
Standard deviation	18.2	14.6

Table 11.2   Statistics of final price of Toys ($n = 100$), comparing shortages and surpluses, money fitness test

Money fitness test	High demand	Low demand
Mean	52.8	49.2
Maximum	405.2	117.8
Minimum	40.9	23.5
Standard deviation	18.2	14.5

increases volatility. The highs are higher, and the lows are lower and the standard deviation, greater. Table 11.2 shows the descriptive statistics after two sets of runs ($n = 100$) of the final price after 3500 iterations. In one run, the system is in shortage (desired Toy inventory = 7) while in the other one, the system is in surplus (desired Toy inventory = 3). The Toy Trader is used instead of the Three-Goods Trader as the price patterns are the same.

In a complex system, supply and demand do impact price, but not the way linear-system theory suggests. Figure 11.3 shows a run of the Toy Trader under an asset fitness test. For the first 500 iterations, the system is in surplus. The next 500 iterations, the system is in shortage. This pattern is then repeated once more. The vertical lines indicate exactly when the change is made.

Figure 11.4 is the same run as Fig. 11.3 except it uses a money fitness test and each section running 3000 iterations (because the money fitness test requires more transactions than an asset fitness test to create their distinctive patterns). Note that without the vertical lines as a guide, it would be nearly impossible to detect exactly when the system went from surplus to shortage. The vertical lines are the same height in Figs. 11.3 and 11.4.

It should be noted that a system with high demand can sometimes experience rapid inflation where the price goes to the maximum possible

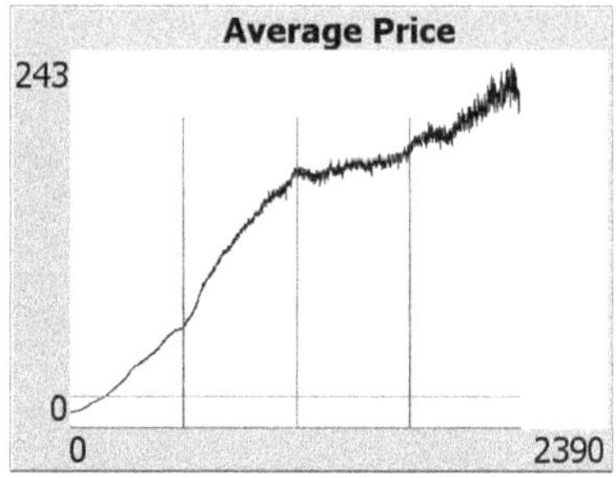

Fig. 11.3 Demand
shocks, asset fitness test

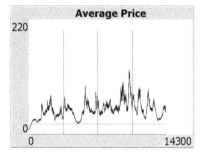

Fig. 11.4 Demand
shocks, money fitness
test

with the given money supply and then get stuck there. This inflation is more probable the longer the system is run while in a shortage
condition.

Overall, supply and demand do impact the market in a complex system, but not in a way that is recognisable from linear-system models and
theory.

Changing supply has very similar effects as demand changes in a sys
tem with evolutionary prerequisites. For example, imagine a government responding to rising house prices by doubling housing supply. In
Fig. 11.5, the Toy Trader starts while supply equals demand (5 toys given
to each agent and 5 toys wanted for inventory). It is run for 1000 iterations and then the supply is doubled by adding 5 toys to each agent's
inventory and run for another 1000 iterations. This is a positive supply shock causing the system to go into surplus. Then a negative supply
shock is applied (subtracting 5 toys from most agents) bringing the system back it original state. The final 1000 iterations are run after a positive
supply shock is applied (adding 5 toys to all agents). The vertical lines in
Fig. 11.5 mark where the supply shocks were applied.

Fig. 11.5 Supply
impacts, asset fitness test

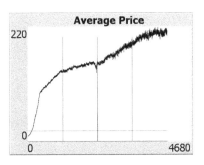

Note that when the Toy Trader is run with homogeneous non-evolutionary agents, supply and demand shocks impact price much as linear system theory suggest.

11.3   Long- and Short-Term Price

There is a body of literature and economic experimentation concerning the double auction (e.g. Easley & Ledyard, 1993; Davis & Holt, 1993; Williams, 1980). This was the basis of a string of economic experiments showing how suppliers seeking profit constrained by cost and buyers constrained by price value will come to a competitive price equilibrium.

For example, if a customer values a product at 120 and the cost to supply it is 20, the supplier will initially offer the price of a product near 120 while the customer will initially bid near 20. As the supplier decreases the price, the customer will increase their bid until the offer and bid meet in the middle. In this example, the settled price will be near 70. This offers a profit of 50 for the supplier $(70 - 20 = 50)$ and an excess value (value minus price paid) of 50 for the customer $(120 - 70 = 50)$. This is the predicted competitive price outcome.

If we build this model as an agent-based model, in the short run, it returns the same results as the experiments reported in the literature. For example, in a simulation run set up as described above, the double-auction model is run for 629 iterations as 100 sellers sold a total of 500 goods to 100 buyers. The last trade took place at a price of 72 with the last bid and offer being 73 and 72, respectively. The price traded is at 72 (not 73) because that is what the supplier was offering.

The price strayed a little from 'equilibrium' (as it did in experiments with people as well) but on the whole, demonstrates the equilibrium and price efficiency that were reported in the double-action literature (Fig. 11.6). This demonstrates that a sound short-run price analysis can be accomplished using linear-system analyses.

In the short run, the double-auction model obeys the linear-system law of supply and demand. If the buyers want more product than is available in the system, price swings upwards before stock runs out. If there is more product available than demand, the price swings downwards before all customers are satiated.

However, if the double-auction model is set up assuming that trade is continuous, meaning that supply and demand are unlimited, a long-run price pattern emerges. When buying and selling are repeated in perpetuity, history takes on a greater importance. The last trading price is the most important piece of information influencing the next trading price. For example, if the price drops $10 (due to a demand drop, perhaps), it is a very different thing when the previous traded price was $1,000,000 compared to $11. The most important piece of data in any market is the last trading price.

The importance of the last trading price reflects the importance of history in economics, but history can take time before its influence is felt. For example, Fig. 11.7 shows the double-auction model running for 500,000 iterations and has unlimited aggregate supply and demand. This would be like suppliers being regularly resupplied while buyers continually consume over time.

The last traded price was 98.21 with bid and offer standing at 101.81 and 98.21, respectively. Note that the price in this simulation is constrained between the buyer's value (because buyers will not buy anything priced higher than their value) and the seller's cost (because sellers will

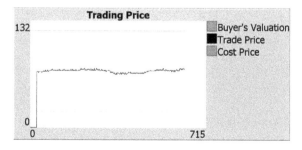

Fig. 11.6   Short-run price in double-auction model

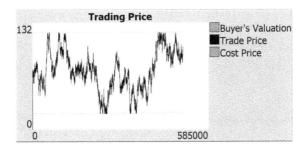

Fig. 11.7   Long-run price in double-auction model, 500,000 iterations

not sell anything below their cost). The price ranges freely between these two hard points. All evidence of equilibria and the implication of pricing efficiency disappear when trading in the double auction persists over the long run.

In the short run, the initial conditions determine the price. All the double-auction experiments start by assuming that consumers know the suppliers' costs and the suppliers know how the consumers' value their product. Then both sides move towards one another at the same over-all rate. This design will inevitably lead to a perfectly competitive initial trade price.

However, price patterns might be predictable. We know that asset prices tend to go up while speculation markets tend to exhibit non-trending volatility. Empirically, both these markets have identifiable evolutionary prerequisites. When these prerequisites are put into a simple trade model, those same price patterns appear.

11.4   SUMMARY

The evolutionary price patterns hold regardless of changes in demand, supply, increasing the number of products, and the pricing algorithms. However, these are the first experiments of this kind and there remains a great deal more to explore in this area.

These results do not impact the normal short-run economic analysis. Experiments using the Double-auction model show how initial conditions are important to the short-run price outcome. It is over time that the initial conditions lose their potency and complex elements, like history, begin to dominate the system. In other words, the standard linear-system economic analysis taught in universities is perfectly adequate in the short run, as this type of analysis is concerned with how initial conditions initially resolve in the system. In the long run, as Veblen (1898) said, perhaps it is time for economics to become an evolutionary science.

REFERENCES

Davis, D. D., & Holt, C. A. (1993). Experimental economics: Methods, problems, and promise. *Estudios Economicos, 8*, 179–212.

Easley, D., & Ledyard, J. O. (1993). Theories of price formation and exchange in double oral auctions. In D. Friedman & J. Rust (Eds.), *The double auction market institutions, theories and evidence* (pp. 63–97). Reading: Addison Wesley.

Veblen, T. (1898). Why is economics not an evolutionary science? *The Quarterly Journal of Economics, 12*(4), 373–397.

Williams, A. W. (1980). Computerized double-auction markets: Some initial experimental results. *Journal of Business, 53*, 235–258.

CHAPTER 12

Factors Impacting Money Distribution

Abstract Relatively efficient evolutionary trade systems were robust in reproducing a money distribution equal to a 0.5 Gini coefficient. This chapter explores the money distribution outcome when trade is inefficient in an evolutionary system. The factors introduced are the number of times an agent attempts trades in a given iteration (trade velocity) and how far the agent can detect price in the market.

Keywords Inequality · Gini coefficient · Market-sight ·
Trade velocity · Endogenous instability · Agent-based models · Toy
Trader · Netlogo · Long-term price · Short-term price

The distribution of the wealth generated by the modern economy is a key factor in the fairness of the economy and society. The key to wealth and resource distribution in a monetary society is the distribution of money. Experiments have shown that heterogeneity alone creates greater inequality, but systems characterised by evolutionary prerequisites demonstrate a strong propensity for money to be distributed at 0.5 Gini. This chapter seeks systemic factors that move money distributions away from a 0.5 Gini coefficient in evolutionary systems.

Two factors will be tested in these experiments: market-sight and number of trades. Market-sight was already tested in non-evolutionary trade in Chapter 10, but all evolutionary experiments so far have been run with market-sight set to 1, the Toy Trader's most efficient setting.

© The Author(s) 2019
T. Gooding, *Economics for a Fairer Society*,
https://doi.org/10.1007/978-3-030-17020-2_12

These experiments test the response of evolutionary systems in less efficient settings.

In addition to market-sight, a new element, number of trades, is tested in these experiments. Up until this point, all agents in the Toy Trader sought to purchase one Toy during each iteration. This is a number of trades setting of 1. If the number of trades is increased so that each agent attempts to buy 2 toys during each iteration, it increases the velocity of trade during each iteration by increasing the frequency of purchases. Note that when an agent becomes too poor, it might only be able to purchase 1 Toy or none.

There is no claim that these results fully represent the modern economy. What is being claimed is that where these prerequisites exist in the actual economy, the trends and tendencies described here will be present in the actual economy even if they are modified by other forces.

This chapter would probably be best understood if the reader ran the models at the suggested settings while reading. The terms here are difficult to grasp without seeing what is happening in the simulation.

12.1   Increasing Number of Trades

Doubling the number of trades does not significantly impact the overall evolutionary patterns. A money fitness test still creates volatile price patterns, while an asset fitness test still generally creates asset price inflation. However, it is possible for the increased volatility to cause the price to race up to a level constrained by the money supply. The higher the number of trades, the higher the price peak. This sudden price inflation has not been observed when the number of trades is set to 1.

In general, increasing the number of trades proportionately creates higher price peaks in the systems with a money fitness test, and steeper slopes in systems with an asset fitness test. Table 12.1 shows the average of the maximum price over 100 runs at four settings of number of

Table 12.1 Average max. price, max. price, fitness test = money, 6000 iteration runs, $n = 100$

Number of trades	1	2	5	10
Ave. max. price over 100 runs	114.2	310.6	427.1	482.8
Max. price over all 100 runs	201.6	783.0	856.2	842.795

trades: 1, 2, 5, 10 (400 total runs). Note that the higher prices would equate to an increased GDP measure.

Perhaps one of the most surprising outcomes of the simulation is how the Gini coefficient of money inversely correlates with price. If prices get above (approximately) 150 in the Toy Trader, the high price depresses the Gini coefficient. If a low price is maintained, the Gini coefficient tends to rise. Table 12.2 shows the weak inverse correlation between price and the Gini coefficient of 10 runs to 6000 iterations. The runs depicted use the money fitness test, market-sight = 1, number of trades = 10.

Figure 12.1 is an example of one of these runs.

Another phenomenon worth noting is that when the number of trades exceeds 1, the system sometimes experiences 'hyperinflation' where prices climb steeply to a level constrained by the money supply. This is evident in the maximum prices from Table 12.1 in all the runs except where number of trades is 1. Before a 'hyperinflation' event, the price pattern is the same as predicted by speculation market evolutionary prerequisites.

Figure 12.2 is an example of 'hyperinflation'. While the price pattern looks to be from an asset fitness test, this system has a money fitness test.

Table 12.2 Price and Gini coefficient correlation of 10 runs, money fitness test, number of trades 10, $n = 6000$

−0.65668	−0.62427	−0.61545	−0.4548	−0.64751
−0.39786	−0.44485	−0.77439	−0.65982	−0.70288

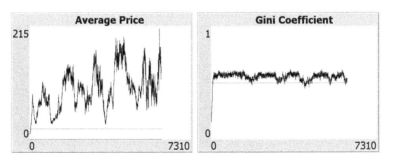

Fig. 12.1 Price and Gini coefficient, number of trades = 10

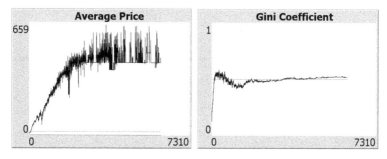

Fig. 12.2   Price and Gini coefficient, 'hyperinflation', number of trades = 3, fitness test = money

In this example, 'hyperinflation' took hold before any other patterns could develop. Note the very high relative price on the *y*-axis.

When the fitness test is changed to assets, the number of trades continues to influence the price peak rather than the shape of the simulation. As was noted in Table 12.1, a strongly rising price results in a slightly lower Gini coefficient. The higher the price, the lower the Gini coefficient. However, even when the number of trades is set to 10, the Gini coefficient of money only goes down to around 0.44. The price patterns retain their characteristic asset price inflation.

Overall, changing the number of trades that each agent is allowed does not significantly alter the established price patterns for each fitness test.

12.2   COMBINING MARKET-SIGHT AND NUMBER OF TRADES

When using a money fitness test, at any market-sight greater than 1, the price races to the bottom and stays there. All resemblance to empirical price patterns disappear. However, increasing the number of trades to 10 restores the realistic price patterns at lower levels of market-sight. The impact is that price patterns run lower and the Gini coefficient higher in accordance to the inverse correlation shown in Table 12.2. Figure 12.3 shows the typical results of Market-sight = 2 and Number of trades = 10.

This trend is magnified if market-sight is increased to 3. The price patterns stay almost exclusively below the reference line set at 20 in the price graph, while the Gini coefficient of money tends to go between 80 and 90.

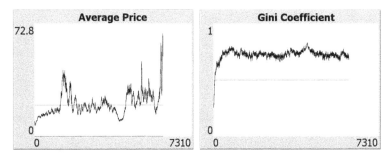

Fig. 12.3 Price and Gini coefficient, number of trades = 10, market-sight = 2, fitness test = money

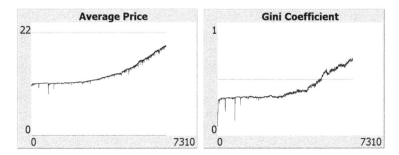

Fig. 12.4 Price and Gini coefficient, number of trades = 1, market-sight = 25, fitness test = assets

Setting market-sight to 3 is as high as the money fitness test system will go in this configuration before the realistic price patterns completely disappear. If market-sight is increased to 4 or beyond, the price drives to the minimum and stays there regardless of the number of trades setting.

The Toy Trader experiments suggest that the asset fitness test is more resilient in the face of increasing market-sight. Overall, increasing the market-sight slows the price adjustment process in proportion to the market-sight increases. The greater the market-sight, the longer it takes for the price to increase (the shallower the slope). Interestingly, the biggest change from increasing market-sight is the increase in inequality of the money distribution. If market-sight is increased to 25 where agents have complete market information, the price increases more slowly and inequality exhibits a marked climb (Fig. 12.4).

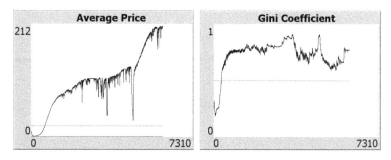

Fig. 12.5 Price and Gini coefficient, number of trades = 10, market-sight = 25, fitness test = assets

The established price patterns are maintained throughout the adjustments of market-sight. This type of system is also resilient to number of trades. For example, if the run shown in Fig. 12.5 (market-sight = 25) is repeated with number of trades set to 10, the charts still exhibit the overall characteristic of asset price inflation (Fig. 12.5), even though the system has become more chaotic.

12.3   THE SPECIAL CASE: NUMBER OF TRADES = 3

When the number of trades is set to 3, the system demonstrates an increased degree of macro instability, especially noticeable when the fitness test is assets.

However, if the inefficiency of the system is increased, the possibility of a macro market 'crash' increases. Consider Fig. 12.6, a simulation run where the market-sight has risen to 10 while the number of trades remains at 3.

After the normally rapid price rise, there is a serious asset price 'crash' evident early in the simulation. This follows a marked increase in wealth inequality alongside with a slow recovery. After the price crash, the price never fully recovers.

To date, this phenomenon has not been seen at any other level of Number of trades. However, even if this phenomenon does appear at a different setting, this phenomenon remains most pronounced when the number of trades is set to 3.

It is tempting to suggest that the apparent chaos exhibited is somehow tied to period 3 system oscillations (Li & Yorke, 1975), as 3 trades

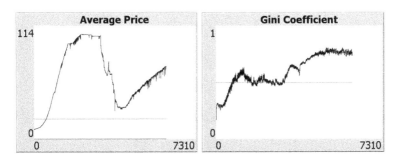

Fig. 12.6 Price and Gini coefficient, number of trades = 3, market-sight = 10, fitness test = assets

occur in one state before a state change takes place through movement. However, there is no evidence (nor a likelihood) that movements return the system to the same state as 3 trades cycles previous. As such, no connection to a period three oscillation can be made at this point. Furthermore, even if it could be demonstrated that setting the simulation to 3 trades somehow equates to period 3 system oscillations, the question remains of how this Toy Trader setting could relate to reality.

Regardless, the fact the Toy Trader destabilises when set to 3 trades is interesting. Furthermore, a market crash, followed by a slow recovery combined with rising inequality is not unknown in the real world. However, nothing further can be said without more research.

12.4   AGENT MOVEMENT

In terms of multi-agent dynamics, altering number of trades impacts the agency of agent movement. The greater the number of trades between agent movements, the less movement is a factor in the simulation dynamics. Were there to be an 'infinite' number of trades between periods of movement, effectively there would be no movement.

Increasing market-sight also acts to diminish the impact of free movement. The greater the market-sight, the less important movement becomes. When market-sight is set to 25, it makes no difference as to whether the agents move at all. Assuming perfect information is one of the agencies that has exorcised time and space from most commonly used economic models.

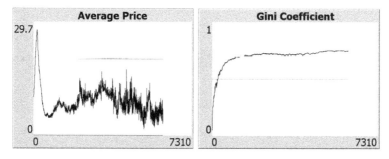

Fig. 12.7 Price and Gini coefficient, money fitness test, agent movement turned off

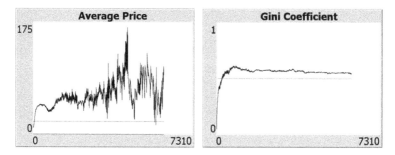

Fig. 12.8 Price and Gini coefficient, asset fitness test, agent movement turned off

As such, the results of the previous experiments suggest that the ability of the agents to move freely is important to the emergent dynamics of trade. This can easily be tested in the Toy Trader by shutting off agent movement. When doing so, Fig. 12.7 shows the most efficient Toy Trader configuration shaped by a money fitness test but with the movement turned off.

As was suggested by the Number-of-Trade experiments (see Fig. 12.3) decreasing movement in a system shaped by a money fitness test causes significant inequality.

It is important to note that these price patterns are not deterministic as they have been in previous runs. The lack of movement and limited visibility creates considerable price volatility. Prices can enter a hyperinflation cycle or race down to the bottom to stay there.

With an asset fitness test, the price stabilises in the middle, it no longer takes on the characteristic asset price inflation shape and in fact becomes quite volatile (Fig. 12.8).

12.5 SUMMARY

Recently, equality has taken on increased importance. To my knowledge, this is the first attempt to explore system characteristics that impact an evolutionary market's wealth distribution. Before this, the economic narrative has been dominated by merit, with the assumption being that everyone could be well-off if they all did what was necessary to be well-off. However, there is building evidence that the physics of a trade system will create pool of impoverished people and small group of highly wealthy individuals, even when the trade system is at its most efficient and everyone has equal talent and effort. Introducing market inefficiencies, such as increased choice, creates greater wealth inequality.

This result suggests that poor people, initially, are not necessarily poor because of their efforts. Nor are the rich necessarily wealthy because of productivity or contributions to society. In other words, we can neither blame the rich nor the poor for their situation.

If society is to be fair, the physics of trade needs to be acknowledged and addressed by policy. As we see in the world today, not doing so is leading us to a very unstable future.

REFERENCE

Li, T. Y., & Yorke, J. A. (1975). Period three implies chaos. *The American Mathematical Monthly, 82*(10), 985–992.

CHAPTER 13

Introducing Life

Abstract While the economic system is meant to serve people, distribution failures present no permanent consequences in linear-system
economic models as endogenously induced starvation and population
changes are not modelled. Metaphoria is an agent-based model that features a 'living' population, one where the agents must find and secure
food in order to remain alive and breed. All their propensities are
evolved, even if this leads to extinction. This enables us to explore starvation and system efficiency in terms of the well-being of the population. It also allows us to directly test the efficiency hypothesis explored in
Chapter 8, as Metaphoria can run a hunter/gather economy and a monetary economy using an identical set of agents in an identical environment.

Keywords Monetary economy · Hunter/gatherer economy ·
Efficiency · Evolution · Evolutionary prerequisites · Inequality ·
Starvation · Population stability · Agent-based model · Netlogo ·
Metaphoria model

An economy's first success is measured by its ability to feed its population. Any economic system that loses this ability renders itself irrelevant,
regardless of any other accomplishments. From an individual's point
of view, the moment there is no food surplus (the term 'food' is being
used to include all necessary sustenance, including water), there is no
free time because any diversion from obtaining food results in death. All

© The Author(s) 2019   125
T. Gooding, *Economics for a Fairer Society*,
https://Doi.org/10.1007/978-3-030-17020-2_13

laziness is ruthlessly evolved out. While there are many ways to die other than starvation, there is no other economic concern that contains this universal consequence for all human beings across the earth.

From this point of view, all activity not devoted to the production and distribution of food is discretionary or leisure time. Society shapes this leisure time into forms we identify as cultural conventions and identity. For example, leisure time could be shaped so that it is customary that we sit in offices for 40 or 50 hours a week. In modern society, we call this 'productive' when compared with chatting with friends, for example, even when those office hours lead to nothing objectively measurable. Modern society also uses its leisure time to go to war with one other. Arguably, the shape of modern society is the outcome of society's evolutionary forces shaping leisure time. Except where the societal shape (or narrative) asks us to kill each other or create a global crisis, the shape of our leisure time is irrelevant to our survival. Keep in mind that before the agricultural revolution 10,000 years ago, human beings suffered almost no disease (Wells, 2010).

It follows that the first and most important aspect of any economy is its ability to produce and distribute food. Logically, this would be the most heavily researched area of our economy. In reality, while the production side of farm activity is highly researched, the consumption side is considered a matter of choice. The assumption is that if anyone wants food badly enough, they will work and get money with which to buy food. Therefore, not having any food is the result of choice, not a systemic outcome. The result is that food presents as another element of leisure in linear-system models, not a biological necessity.

In fact, most modern economic theory restricts itself to the analysis and optimisation of society's products of leisure. Key stated concerns are economic growth, innovation, monetary efficiency, and profit maximisation. Economic models are designed to explore and understand these phenomena using linear-system methods combined with historical empirics (econometrics). The baseline assumptions of these models are that price accurately reflects long-term supply and demand, profits (wealth) indicate economic success, and economic success indicates societal success.

In currently dominant economic models, food is simply one more commodity used to generate profits and add to the GDP. In such models, there are no consequences of trade reduction other than a 'financial crisis', another one of society's leisure activities. The Kenyan cartoonist Mwampembwa (2008) noticed this when he depicted rich capitalists frantically running around screaming 'Crisis!' while citizens of Kenya living a subsistence life were baffled by the commotion. A Kenyan man listens to a portable radio and asks: '...crisis, what crisis!?' Linear-system models measure the consequences of the financial crisis horror in performance issues such as lower profits and higher unemployment. Nowhere is there concern for the poor in terms of food distribution.

Assuming that all economic activity beyond food is society's leisure supports a logical argument sounding much like Marx's labour theory of value (Marx & Ryazanskaya, 1963). First, replace Marx's labour with societal leisure. Without leisure time, there is no excess labour with which productive capital can be created or utilised. With leisure time, labour becomes available to create capital wealth. Capital accumulation is not a prerequisite, it is the result of societal leisure time. Therefore, it can be argued that labour, converted from human leisure, is the origin of all modern economic value beyond food. Therefore, anyone receiving a larger share of society's wealth arising from capital or labour could be seen as 'exploiting' the converted leisure time because in order for someone to receive more of the fruits of society's leisure, others necessarily receive less than the true value of their leisure labour.

Of course, many argue that those 'exploiting' the labour of workers are in fact directly responsible for the increased 'leisure' time available in today's first world economies. As Friedman and his followers suggest, if everyone is better off, it does not matter that the benefit may be unequally distributed (Friedman, 1976). The assumption underlying these arguments is that the power differential created by wealth inequality is beneficial to society, as wealthy people demonstrably embody better productive practices than less wealthy people. Therefore, it is best for society to have productive people controlling a larger share of society's resources.

However, Friedman's wisdom does not include understandings from complex system. In a complex system, prices are not long-term indicators of supply and demand (Chapter 10). If price is disconnected from supply and demand, then it is not an indicator of the desires of society. Therefore, if wealth is obtained through trading using price, then wealth is not connected with productivity. As was seen in Chapter 8, a wealthy elite will arise from systemic causes built into the free-market system.

After hundreds of years of capitalism, a significant portion of the world continues to go without enough food. This is true even in the oldest free-market economies such as the UK. The starvation rate is currently rising due to 'austerity' measures. Unless we agree that lower productivity is a crime punishable by death, then there is something deadly wrong with the modern free-market economy.

It is important to note that this work is not an indictment of the wealthy. Today, the free-market system is supported in principle by rich and poor alike. What this research indicates is that a free market will inevitably create a small class of super-rich people, even if the entire population has equal skill and equal opportunity. This is not the fault of the rich. What this research suggests is that the magnitude of the richest peoples' success is due to systemic forces rather than their clever strategies. In a nutshell, the world as we see it today is mostly the result of the system that is dominant in human society, not the cunning or the 'selfishness' of the wealthy, or the lack or 'laziness' of the poor.

Regardless, it is an empirical fact that in modern society, wealth inequality kills people. The next model, Metaphoria, explores systemic origin of wealth inequality in a complex system and its impact on a mortal population, that is a population that requires food to remain alive and must reproduce to stay present.

13.1   METAPHORIA

Metaphoria is the simplest economic model I could think to build using a mortal population. Failure to feed oneself means death. Failure to successfully reproduce means extinction.

In models where it is impossible for agents to develop behaviour leading to extinction, the population is a model artefact, programmed a priori to be present. In this case, key emergent forces that support or repress life remain hidden.

The agents in Metaphoria are free to evolve their behaviour in any direction they choose, including towards behaviour that leads to extinction. In Metaphoria, evolutionary pressures are necessary to keep the agents alive. However, if a dominant fitness test emerges that is not tied to life, such as profit or wealth, then the creation of self-destructive social tendencies becomes possible.

Metaphoria is several orders of magnitude more complex than the Toy Trader model. It would take months to fully explain everything learnt from Metaphoria and similar models. As Railsback and Grimm (2011, p. 9) point out that, 'while new modellers might think that designing a model and implementing it on the computer takes most of the work, this task – analyzing a model and learning from it – is the most time-consuming and demanding one'.

Metaphoria can simulate the economic organisations of the equivalent of hunter/gatherer and monetary economic organisations. Each society can be initiated with identical agents in identical positions in identical environments. Thus, two societal organisations can be compared directly. Technology has not yet been programmed into Metaphoria's monetary society. However, the premise that free-trade markets are the most efficient economic organisation can be tested directly.

Note that in measuring economic efficiency, aggregate economic production is not what is being compared. Today's free-market economy uses vast energies to power planet-changing economic activity (Garrett, 2014). The free market is the undisputed king of throughput, but is it an efficient economic organisation?

13.2   Building a Mortal Population

Building a self-determining mortal population in Netlogo (or any agent-based model) is relatively simple. The environment is set up so that it contains a resource that the agents require to live. This resource equates to food and water. Movement allows the agents to find the resources. Agents all possess 'labour' that is used to harvest the needed resource. If enough is harvested, children are born and fed until they reach adulthood. The model allows for sexual or asexual reproduction, though experimentation suggests that it does not make much of a difference to economic patterns.

What makes this population interesting is the agents' ability to choose their own behaviour. All behaviour is based on propensities that are evolved, as it was when the Toy Trader evolved pricing behaviour. The agent has a certain probability of doing something, such as having a child. Whatever the behaviours the parent(s) has are passed onto whatever children they give birth to, though the behaviour can sometimes mutate. In the real world, parents of teenagers sometimes call this 'rebellion'. The fitness test in this case is remaining alive and reproducing instead of wealth or success.

The only thing constraining the behaviour is realism. For example, in the real world, an agent cannot have negative biological fertility. Therefore, the programming limits fertility variables from evolving to negative numbers. Otherwise, agents are free to evolve their fertility to any level they wish, including no fertility. The simulation begins with heterogeneous agents initialised with randomly generated fertility variables. Once the simulation is running, evolution takes over. Regardless of how fertile an agent may be, there is an upper limit to actual reproduction that matches that of human beings. The assumption is that approximately half the population is female and that the fastest reproduction that can take place is approximately 1 child per female per year. As this population does not use males and females, a single agent can have a maximum of 1 child every two years.

Those unfamiliar with evolution might think that the result would simply be a race among the agents to be the most fertile. However, this simplistic notion of 'survival of the fittest' is not how evolution works. In the long term, successful populations do not overpopulate their environment. In fact, during a prolonged population explosion, the model's population frequently exhibits declining fertility variables, just as is happening in the human population today (Jensen, Andersen, & Skakkebæk, 2004; Lutz, Testa, & Penn, 2006).

Individual agent propensities determine how and whether an agent will look for food or stay in one place, reproduce, feed their child, save food, etc. All agent behaviours are governed by evolved variables that drive propensities. If a variable is unimportant, charts of that variable result in stochastic walks. Where variables are important, repeatable patterns appear forged by emergent behaviour and/ or evolution. Through repeated testing of many different variables, it becomes apparent which variables are important and which ones are not. When several evolved variables take on patterns that match the patterns of empirical data, the simulation is considered a success (Grimm et al., 2005).

All the agents' evolved variables are initially randomly generated. In the first few generations, agents possessing unviable behavioural characteristics die out. Then the system settles down and starts improving their evolutionary fitness.

The only agent variables not evolved in this model are their maximum labour and their requirement for food. In these terms, the agents are homogeneous. These two key agent variables act in an environment that is initiated with two randomly generated variables representing food and resistance to harvesting. All agents on the same patch combine their labour to overcome the resistance and harvest the food.

Three Examples of Harvesting

Agent settings for all three examples:
- Minimum food requirement per iteration 2.1.
- Labour per iteration 5.

Patch 1: Food present 8, Resistance 1
- One agent can harvest 4 food ((5 labour—1 resistance) to a maximum of 8) every iteration.
- Two agents can harvest 4 food each (10 labour—1 resistance) to a maximum of 8. Divide harvest by two agents.
- Three agents can harvest (8 food/3 agents) 2.66 each.
- Four agents can harvest 2 each. All would be in danger of starvation if they stayed.

Patch 2: Food present 3, Resistance 3
- One agent can harvest 2. It would starve.
- Two agents can harvest 1.5 each. Both would starve. This is a barren patch.

Patch 3: Food present 8, Resistance 8
- One agent cannot harvest anything.
- Two agents can harvest 2 (1 food each). Both will starve.
- Three agents can harvest 7 (2.33 food each). All will survive.
- Four agents can harvest 8 (2 food each). All will starve.

The agents have no means to detect one another. All they recognise is whether they are getting enough food or not.

Some agents have a higher propensity to explore and risk starvation by venturing out into the unknown to look for more productive patches. This enables the population to expand into its environment. An agent unable to find a harvestable food patch will die of starvation.

Agents have a user-set maximum life term set at approximately 85 years in these simulation runs. After 85, the agent has a 1 in 7 chance of dying of old age on every subsequent iteration. If an agent dies after hitting this age, it will be considered to have died from old age and charted accordingly.

Agents tend to feed their children unless their own starvation is threatened. If a parent dies, the children may or may not survive to maturity depending on its stock of food and, in the monetary system, how much money it has.

While this is not the main thrust of this work, this model broadly obeys the laws of thermodynamics. The most important energy activities, such as requiring food for life and reproduction, is accounted for. Where it fails is that where agents engage in higher computation. There has been no energy cost assigned to this activity. Also, if an agent is idle, there is no food requirement reduction. The energy accounting for a 'technological' society is represented in the Gooding (2014) model.

13.3   HUNTER/GATHERER ECONOMY

The fitness test of the hunter/gatherer society is survival. Agents harvest food from the environment and then share their harvest with those on the same patch. The key organising principle here is emergent behaviour, the same principle that organises beehives, ant nests, or allows termites to build elaborate and efficient buildings (Bonabeau, Dorigo, & Theraulaz, 1999). Each agent requires very little computational power to participate in an emergent system. In accordance with the Rand/Stonedahl hypothesis (see Chapter 9), the hunter/gatherer society is predicted to be relatively efficient.

Figure 13.1 shows a hunter/gatherer society run at the following settings:

- Patches—food between 0 and 50, resistance between 0 and 37.
- Agents—food requirement 2.4, labour 5.

Charts

- **Birth and Death**—Charts the birth rate and the death rate on the same chart. The middle horizontal line is 0 for both charts. The birth rate is positively charted above the 0 line by summing all births and dividing by the population in the previous

---

iteration. The death rate is negatively charted below the 0 line and sums all deaths and divides by the population in the previous iteration. There are two light horizontal reference lines set at 0.5 and −0.5.

- **Longevity**—Sums the age reached by all agents who died during that iteration and divides by the number of deaths. A horizontal reference line is set to 45.
- **Cause of Death**—Tracks how the agents are dying. The lighter line sums all the agents who died because of starvation and divides by the population. The black line sums all the deaths due to old age and divides by the population.

Note the high level of the population. The simulation runs quite slowly at these levels.

The system evolves starvation downwards while longevity exhibits a steady rise to a level recognisable as a human life span. Also, note the stability of the system. Even if we significantly lower the available resources

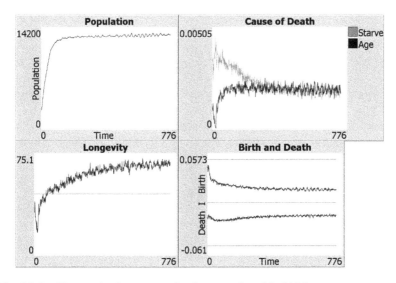

Fig. 13.1   Hunter/gatherer, max food per patch = 52, 3000 years

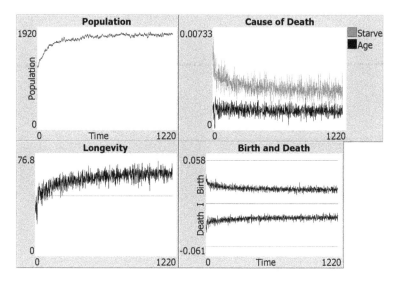

Fig. 13.2   Hunter/gatherer, max food per patch = 10, 3000 years

in the environment so that the maximum food possible on a patch is 10 (Fig. 13.2), the chart patterns remain the same. The main difference is the lower population level.

The key point here is that when adding more energy (whether food or power) to a system, except at key tipping points, the energy difference simply alters the size of the system. For example, if there is starvation in the system, adding more food does not stop starvation, it simply allows for a bigger version of the same system with a similar starvation rate.

One notable characteristic generating a stable society is the stable birth and death rate. Note how the Birth and Death graphs from both runs exhibit smooth parallel shapes.

13.4   MONETARY SYSTEM ECONOMY

A monetary system model asks more computational power of its agents and the system compared to one organised by emergent behaviour. Instead of the simple behavioural rules of emergence, an agent in a monetary system must repeatedly check and compare prices to make decisions. Each new choice requires additional computational resources.

Accordingly, the Rand/Stonedahl hypothesis (see Chapter 9) predicts the monetary system will be significantly less efficient.

In Metaphoria, businesses adjust their offered wages according to the productivity and worker availability. There was a plan to introduce a profit fitness test to businesses, but it has not yet been implemented.

Businesses sell their goods and adjust their prices according to profitability and stock levels. If the business starts losing money, they raise their selling price and lower their wages. If stock gets too high, they start laying workers off as long as their resulting workforce is sufficient to harvest the food. If their workforce drops below the minimum required to harvest, they raise their wage offers. If a business completely sells out of stock, they raise their prices. Prices and wages are raised and lowered in a similar manner as those in the evolutionary Toy Trader model (see Chapter 10) though the algorithms are more complex. The exact integers used in the price up and price down movements are dictated to the business by the agent that owns the business. These agent variables control business experience mutation but, as mentioned before, are not directly under the influence of a profitability fitness test.

Two points must be emphasised. One is that Metaphoria is a work-in-progress. There are many ways prices and wages can be handled and while some have been explored, there are innumerable methods that have not. The second point is that the exact detail of price and wage handling is frequently not as important to the shape of the results as one might think. As was demonstrated in Chapters 10 and 11, the shape of the prices tends to be dictated by the evolutionary forces in play.

The evolutionary forces in a monetary society will arise from money. Agents with a lot of money thrive while those without do not. This makes money (or wealth) the fitness test that will shape the system. Note that a money fitness test has nothing to do with life, productivity, or societal health. Therefore, we should not expect the monetary system to outperform the hunter/gatherer society in terms of population health.

The simulation is initiated with no money at all. If a business does not have enough money to pay its wages, it first gets money from the 'Central Bank' that has not obligations, but once a user-set amount of money is in circulation, it must borrow money. Loan terms are user-set. For these runs, the loans were either non-repayable and free or they were set at only 0.4% of the principal payable each business cycle and the interest set to only 0.3%. If a business does not have the funds to make a loan payment, it can take out another loan with no restrictions. The way this simulation is currently set up, a business can never go bankrupt or run out of money.

With loan repayments turned on, the money supply can sometimes fluctuate. Over the long term, money supply grows exponentially at a rate typically between 0.5 and 1% per year. This is considerably below the money supply growth rate of many of today's real economies. If all loan repayments are turned off, the long-term money supply grows at a rate typically between 2 and 3% per year. Regardless of these low growth figures, money is the variable that typically forces the simulation run to stop because otherwise, the numbers grow so large that Netlogo (version 6.0) stops graphing.

The money supply is monitored to ensure that system-wide debits and credits always add up to 0 and that money is not 'leaking' in the model. In Post-Keynesian parlance, it is stock-flow consistent.

Businesses are formed when an agent finds a fertile patch without any businesses on it. The business receives all its behaviour attributes from the owner-agent. If a business makes enough of a profit, the owner-agent receives a dividend. If business activity stops, the business closes. If anything is left in the accounts or the store, it is given to the owner-agent of that business.

The agents themselves simply respond to market signals. They look for jobs within a user-adjustable range that offers the highest wage. They look for goods within their user-adjustable range that asks the lowest selling price. Agents do not buy goods from each other; they only purchase from shops. While hunter/gatherer agents do not need sight to survive, if monetary agents have too small a range, they struggle to survive. Keep in mind how range influenced the efficiency of the system (see Sect. 9.3).

The maximum movement of agents is usually constrained by their sight, though they do have an evolved exploratory propensity where they can travel further out. They also have an evolved propensity to quit work and gamble on finding a better wage.

With respect to labour, food needs, reproduction, and old age, the agents are identical to that of the hunter/gatherer population. So is the environment. Both the population and the environment are seeded during the set-up so that the stochastic processes of set-up create an identical population starting in an identical environment.

The money distribution chapter demonstrated how money tends to distribute itself to a Gini coefficient of 0.5. If this holds true in Metaphoria, starvation will feature in the monetary economy because the poorest agents in the exponential wealth distribution will be unable to

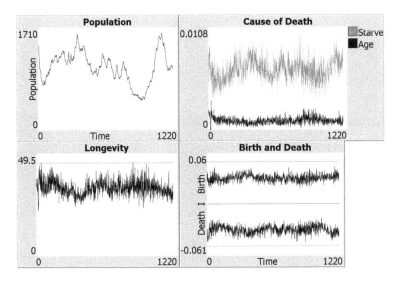

Fig. 13.3 Monetary economy, 3000 years, environment identical to Fig. 13.1

afford food. The impact of starvation on the fitness test was specifically explored in Sect. 6.4.

Figure 13.3 shows the demographic charts from the monetary society using the identical environment and agent population as Fig. 13.1. This is not an attempt to match historical trends, as was Gooding (2014), but rather an exploration of the impact of a monetary economic organisation on a mortal population. Just as with Fig. 13.1, Fig. 13.3 is run to 3000 years. Note the population levels compared to those in Fig. 13.1.

Fig. 13.4 Gini coefficient of money of Fig. 13.3

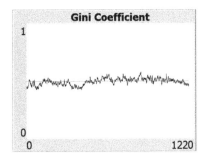

This economy is driven by money and exhibits a higher level of starvation, lower longevity and chaotic nature of the system in general when compared to the emergent economic system. One chart that is not chaotic is the distribution of money. At these settings, money tends to go towards a distribution of 0.5 on the Gini coefficient (Fig. 13.4).

Perhaps the most optimistic chart is that of the GDP which is calculated by summing the (price × quantities) of all trades (except wages) during each iteration. Though not shown, when graphed logarithmically, it becomes nearly straight line with a few 'bumps' in it. However, the optimistic GDP hides a flaw: this system is fundamentally unstable. Unseeding the random number generator on set-up allows different populations to be generated in different environments. It is not uncommon for these systems to go extinct even though there is plenty of food (Fig. 13.5).

If the food is reduced to a level in which the hunter/gatherer population still thrives (Fig. 13.2), the monetary economy population in these simulations immediately goes extinct. These results are consistent with the Rand/Stonedahl hypothesis concerning the link between system efficiency and agent computational effort (see Chapter 9).

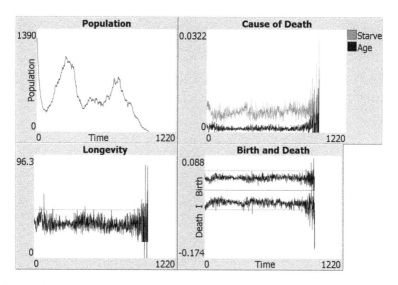

Fig. 13.5   Extinction in year 2494

13.5   SURPLUS FOOD AND STARVATION

In the real world, energy technology has vastly increased society's food supply. As a result, human beings are experiencing the greatest population explosion in our history. The impact of technology in food production can be simulated by manually increasing the food supply in Metaphoria. The following simulation run (Fig. 13.6) shows a 400-year simulation run when resistance to harvesting has been set to 0 and food potential for each patch increased from 52 to 175.

Charts

Food per Capita—Sums all the food held by agents and divides by the population.

Per Capita Productivity—Sums all the food harvested during an iteration and divides by the adult population. A horizontal reference line is set at 0.6.

The relatively high starvation rate is backed by empirical evidence. In 2001, the UN published a report roughly calculating the starvation rate in the world at that time. Of everyone born on earth, the percentage who would die from the effects of starvation was estimated to be 58%

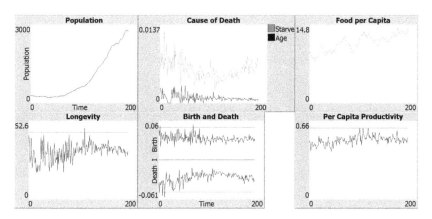

Fig. 13.6   Monetary economy, maximum food per patch 200, no resistance

(Ziegler, 2002). Note that this statistic does not suggest that 58% of the world population dies every year from starvation. People not starving tend to live longer than those who do. A starving population will die more quickly and necessarily reproduce at a higher rate to stay present. Therefore, a starving population will contribute more to the death rate than a healthy population of equal numbers.

It must be emphasised that no one followed up on this report to confirm, deny, or to enhance this work. Today, there are no current data concerning the world starvation rate or trends of the world starvation. We can only infer the possibility of death due to starvation from data collected from organisations such as the World Food Programme (World Food Programme, n.d.): 'In a world where we produce enough food to feed everyone, **795 million people – one in nine – still go to bed on an empty stomach each night**. Even more – one in three – suffer from some form of malnutrition' (emphasis original).

Similar results are seen in the simulation. A relatively high starvation rate continues in the presence of abundant food. Figure 13.6 exhibits climbing per capita food stores as the starvation rate continues to climb as is the case in the real world. This strongly suggests that starvation in the simulator and the world is a problem of distribution, not production. This suggests that attempting to solve world hunger by increasing food production will not abate the starvation in a global free-market economic organisation. Instead, it will simply facilitate an increased rate of growth in the human population.

Overall, these experimental conclusions support recent results from genetic anthropology. According to our genetic records, human beings were relatively disease-free and, except for issues around childbirth, long-lived (Wells, 2010). In fact, there are certain measures of health, such as the Pelvic Inlet Depth Index, where we still have not caught up to our hunter/gatherer ancestors from 10,000 years ago (ibid., p. 23). Similarly, an emergent economic organisation leads to a much healthier and more stable society than a monetary economic system shaped by a wealth fitness test.

Note the global fitness test present in modern global society. Rich people are empowered, and poor people are disempowered. This leads to a global wealth aggregation fitness test (Gooding, 2014). The astute reader will notice that a wealth aggregation fitness test has no links to the well-being of society, the environment, health, or individual people. This is evident in many areas such as in the natural systems of the earth where over half of all wildlife has disappeared since 1970 (WWF/ZSL, 2016) and in a world with an abundant food supply, millions of people are starving to death.

Some suggest that this conclusion is obvious to most people and hardly requires papers, arguments, or experiments to prove it. However, it is important to remember that evolution can solve problems in a manner that is generally incomprehensible to people. The presence of these evolutionary prerequisites makes it likely we are living in a society characterised where evolutionary solutions continuously evolve society's structure to facilitate wealth concentration over all other considerations, including human life.

One possible criticism is that this is not a new insight. Many people already argue that wealth accumulation and its accompanying power are the most important thing in modern society. The point of this work is not to 'discover' this societal characteristic, but to suggest a physical root cause that does not rely on an interpretation of 'human nature'. Furthermore, if society's evolutionary prerequisites are the root cause, then the only way to conclusively solve this problem is to directly address these prerequisites and change the global fitness test to something other than wealth concentration. Otherwise, policy-makers will be faced with the challenge of out-planning an evolutionary system capable of producing extra-generational solutions that have been demonstrated to operating beyond human understanding (Hillis, 1999).

13.6   SUMMARY

This research claims to capture the tendency in a monetary economy towards impoverishment even in the presence of abundance. There is no claim that the empirical level of starvation in the world has been replicated. Of course, starvation is simply the ultimate manifestation of impoverishment. The overall claim of this research is that the systemic forces underlying monetary trade in a complex system will result in the emergence of a poverty class and a rich class, even among agents with homogeneous skills and ability.

If money is the only way to get food, and money is unevenly distributed, food deprivation will result even in the presence of large quantities of food. The tendency for money to distribute itself to a 0.5 Gini coefficient was shown to hold in more complex market simulations where money is not conserved. Accordingly, the agents caught on the wrong side of the exponential money distribution cannot get food in a market economy. This is what the Metaphoria model reflects.

Furthermore, the efficiency of the market economy is negatively influenced by the computation effort required by its agents when compared to simpler economies, such as hunter/gatherer societies. Note that when the anthropologist Sahlins (2017) made a study of the Australian indigenous people living in desert conditions, he discovered that they worked approximately 3–5 hours a day. The rest of the time was used for socialising, exploration, and games. In other words, indigenous people have surplus that they converted into leisure.

The market economy also has a lot of surplus, but that surplus is being converted into things and services in such a way that most common workers experience relatively little leisure surplus. In a modern economy, the other extreme is empty leisure through lack of work and lack of money, because modern leisure time is not worth a great deal without leisure money to go with it. For an indigenous person, food, travel, and clothing is available to anyone. In a modern economy, a totally fit intelligent person can be trapped because they do not have enough money to eat, or travel, or clothe themselves. This is not efficient. While price-allocated resources may succeed in generating profits (especially as the market prerequisites are those necessary to cause society to create evolutionary solutions for greater profits), the evidence suggests that profit does not necessarily produce well-being for the population as a whole.

This result is empirically supported by the relatively high levels of food deprivation in the modern world despite the presence of abundant food. When the model imitates technological advances in farming by raising the availability of food, the population rises while maintaining elevated starvation levels. This is what the world experienced throughout the twentieth century.

References

Bonabeau, E., Dorigo, M., & Theraulaz, G. (1999). *Swarm intelligence: From natural to artificial systems* (No. 1). Oxford: Oxford University Press.

Friedman, M. (1976). *Price theory*. New York: Aldine.

Garrett, T. J. (2014). Long-run evolution of the global economy: 1. Physical basis. *Earth's Future, 2*(3),127–151.

Gooding, T. (2014). Modelling society's evolutionary forces. *Journal of Artificial Societies and Social Simulation, 17*(3), 3.

Grimm, V., Revilla, E., Berger, U., Jeltsch, F., Mooij, W. M., Railsback, S. F., …, & DeAngelis, D. L. (2005). Pattern-oriented modeling of agent-based complex systems: Lessons from ecology. *Science, 310*(5750), 987–991. https://doi.org/10.1126/science.

Hillis, W. D. (1999). *The pattern on the stone: The simple ideas that make computers work.* New York City: Basic Books.

Jensen, T. K., Andersen, A. N., & Skakkebæk, N. E. (2004, April). Is human fertility declining? In *International congress series* (Vol. 1266, pp. 32–44). Amsterdam: Elsevier.

Lutz, W., Testa, M. R., & Penn, D. J. (2006). Population density is a key factor in declining human fertility. *Population and Environment, 28*(2), 69–81.

Marx, K., & Ryazanskaya, S. (1963). *Theories of surplus-value: Volume IV of Capital.* Moscow: Foreign Languages Publishing House.

Mwampembwa, G. (2008, October 27, Monday). What financial crisis? *Daily Nation,* Kenya.

Railsback, S. F., & Grimm, V. (2011). *Agent-based and individual-based modeling: A practical introduction.* Princeton: Princeton University Press.

Sahlins, M. (2017). *Stone age economics.* Abingdon: Routledge.

Wells, S. (2010). *Pandora's seed: Why the hunter/gatherer holds the key to our survival.* London: Penguin Books.

World Food Programme. (n.d.). *Zero hunger.* Retrieved June 16, 2017, from http://www1.wfp.org/zero-hunger.

WWF/ZSL. (2016). *Living planet index database.* WWF and Zoological Society of London. Retrieved from www.livingplanetindex.org.

Ziegler, J. (2002). *The right to food: Report by the special rapporteur on the right to food (Mr. Jean Ziegler).* Submitted in accordance with Commission on Human Rights resolution 2001/25. Addendum, UN: Mission to Niger.

CHAPTER 14

Long-Term Economic Outcome

Abstract It is a fact that using a 'living' population in a model introduces a number of complexities. But is this complication necessary for a sound economic analysis? Common sense tells us that the economy will affect the population, and the population will affect the economy. This chapter explores the outcome of identical processes applied to eternal agents (those used in almost all other economic models) and that of 'living' population. The experiments show that introducing a living population shifts several economic graphs. This result suggests that long-term economic outcomes or narratives cannot be determined with confidence in models using eternal agents or eternal populations.

Keywords Living agents · Eternal agents · Long-term economic outcomes · Evolution · Mutation · Evolutionary prerequisites · Agent-based model · Netlogo · Metaphoria model

The experimental question of this chapter is simple: do predicted long-term economic trends change if eternal populations are replaced by mortal populations in economic models? This is important because the factors to which we ascribe building a good future determine our experience today. If our economic narrative is incorrect, we could be shaping our society in an entirely inappropriate manner for what we want in the future.

Linear-system macroeconomic models tend to use representative agents (Hartley, 2002). In these models, life is assumed a priori, meaning that the economic analysis begins with the assumption that all agents possess the means to perpetually live in addition to a surplus with which to trade. Specifically, in these models, poverty does not lead to death. Policy-makers using such models are blind to a visceral human reality.

With the caveat that comprehensive search for all ABMs in all working papers, academic disciplines, and industry is difficult, except for a version of Sugarscape (Epstein & Axtell, 1996), economic agent-based models use eternal populations—models populated by undying populations. For example, in a recent book about agent-based modelling in economics, of 19 economic models presented in the book, 'Some models have just two agents, but most have a 1000 and largest has 10001' (Hamill & Gilbert, 2016, p. 234). This indicates that the agent populations are predetermined and eternal.

There is nothing intrinsically wrong with building and learning from economic models that assume life. However, perspective is important. Where life is assumed, trade is reduced to a game that we play where the jeopardy is simply ending up with less than the winner.

Developing long-term economic theory and policy recommendations using models that assume life is only be suitable if the outcome of such models is the same as those with mortal populations. If significant differences appear, then long-term theory-building and policy design require mortal agents. Otherwise, serious theory and policy errors could result.

14.1   COMPARING HUNTER/GATHERER WITH TRADE ECONOMY DYNAMICS

In Metaphoria, there is a switch that allows users to turn agent mortality on and off. When on, the agents must use money to solve the problems of sustenance and reproduction. Just as in the real world, if an agent stops eating for long enough, they die. When mortality is turned off, the agents never die and never need to reproduce. Life is assumed.

Note the experimental question is: to what degree do mortal populations change the long-term outcome in economics models? There are no claims as to the empirical accuracy of long-term predictions. While it is interesting how the chart patterns change, except for starvation, no research has been done establishing to what degree these changes reflect reality.

As was done in the previous chapter, the random number generator is seeded so that each pair of simulation runs begins with identical populations in identical environments. However, it is impossible to keep the populations the same throughout the run. In the 'live' scenario, the overall agent population is changing in size as well as evolving and adapting. The eternal agents remain unchanged throughout the model run, just as is the case in most economic models used for theory and policy development.

Charts

GDP—Sums the total price of all trades for each iteration.

Unemployment—Sums the number of adult agents without a job and divides by the total number of adults, and then multiplies by 100 to get a percentage.

Per Capita Productivity—This sums the total physical harvest (real harvest) in the system and divides by the population. There is a horizontal reference line set to 0.6.

Gini Coefficient—This is set to measure money only for these runs in order to further test this distribution (see Chapter 8). There is a horizontal reference line set at 0.5.

Wage/Price Ratio—The average system wage divided by the average system price.

Profit Rate—For all businesses, the amount of money in their account in the previous iteration is divided by the amount of money in the current iteration to create a profit rate. The figure graphed is the average profit rate of all businesses.

Figure 14.1 shows the economic graphs from a mortal population through the equivalent of 3000 years. These patterns at not as deterministic as the runs in the Toy Trader. However, their broad patterns remain consistent.

Figure 14.2 is the identical run with identical initial condition. The only change is the introduction to a mortal population.

When comparing these graphs, it is important to keep an eye on the magnitude of the *y*-axis number. The mortal population has a higher unemployment rate, lower wage/price ratio, productivity is lower,

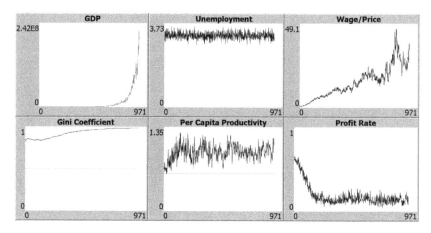

Fig. 14.1   Economic charts, eternal population, 2300 years

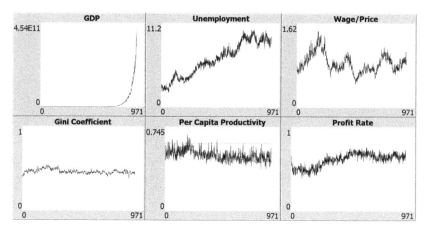

Fig. 14.2   Economic charts, mortal population, 2300 years

business profit rates are higher, and a 0.5 Gini coefficient of money has reappeared. These are the trends apparent in repeatedly running the simulation at these settings. Table 14.1 is the statistic of the final number from these six charts over 50 eternal population runs and 43 mortal population runs (Table 14.2).

The reason for only 43 mortal runs (n=43) is that 7 populations went extinct and were removed from the statistics. Even so, the enormous standard deviation of the mortal population GDP indicates that at least one of these populations was in the process of going extinct but had not quite done so.

The results suggest that using a mortal population significantly alters the long-term outcomes of an economic model. Specific to Metaphoria, the Wage/Price Ratio tends to be higher and the Profit Rate lower in the simulation runs with eternal agents. The eternal agents also demonstrate consistently higher Per Capita Productivity and their unemployment rate tend to be lower. Interestingly, one of the key economic performance measures, GDP, is higher in the mortal populations than the eternal ones. This is likely the result of the mortal population's ability to grow. However, the choice of an eternal population of 1000 agents was made after taking several averages of population levels of mortal runs in order to best equate the two runs.

The graph demonstrating the largest contrast is the Gini coefficient. In the simulation runs featuring eternal agents, the Gini coefficient is just under 1. However, in the eternal population, the agents are heterogeneous and not evolving. This is a similar outcome to that in Sect. 10.2.1, where it was demonstrated that heterogeneity increases inequality.

Table 14.1 Descriptive statistics, eternal agents, 50 runs to 2300 years ($n=50$)

Eternal	GDP	Unemployment	Wage/price	Gini	Productivity	Profit rate
Mean	443,886,826	3.5646	25.03612	0.98496	0.940276	0.171254
Standard deviation	694,136,541	0.402219	7.285399	0.005489	0.089053	0.091889
Min.	19,673,618	2.62	11.83577	0.962788	0.783058	0.028189
Max.	4,231,152,383	4.39	46.11151	0.993367	1.120087	0.492184

Table 14.2 Descriptive statistics, mortal agents, 43 runs to 2300 years ($n=43$)

Mortal	GDP	Unemployment	Wage/price	Gini	Productivity	Profit rate
Mean	88,631,297,726	5.893513	0.93025	0.432144	0.448054	0.517081
Standard deviation	242,783,000,000	3.95908	0.398724	0.062892	0.070005	0.220716
Min.	9441.10577	0.444769	0.256305	0.261309	0.254512	−0.01753
Max.	1,517,250,000,000	14.37223	2.098387	0.532326	0.593505	0.803986

However, heterogeneity alone was not the cause of the extreme inequality evident in the eternal population.

14.2   BANK PROFITS AND WEALTH EQUALITY

In Metaphoria, money is created either by a central agency without interest, or by banks who charge interest. Where money is created by banks, interest becomes an instrument to siphon off wealth from the economy. In the long run, this leads to extreme wealth inequality. This can be demonstrated in Metaphoria by setting interest rates to 0%.

Turning off loan interest directly impacts the shape and level of the Gini Coefficient when using eternal populations. Interestingly, it also stabilises the mortal population, and extinctions decrease in frequency. Figure 14.3 shows the charts from an eternal population run without interest or loan repayments, and Fig. 14.4 shows the mortal population run. Note that the interest rates in the previous runs were set very low: 0.3% interest on loans with repayments set to 0.4%.

Tables 14.3 and 14.4 show the descriptive statistics of the above charts at the end of 50 runs. Three mortal populations went extinct in this series.

Note the GDP of mortal populations can vary tremendously because of positive feedback with money supply and a strong correlation with population levels. On the other hand, GDP of eternal populations is

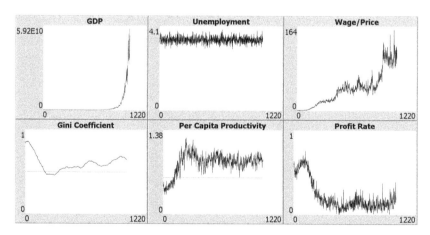

Fig. 14.3   Economic charts, eternal population, no interest

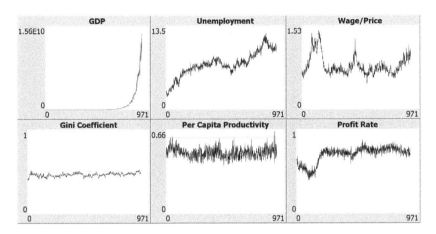

Fig. 14.4   Economic charts, mortal population, no interest

Table 14.3   Eternal agents, no interest, 50 runs to 2300 years ($n=50$)

Eternal	GDP	Unemployment	Wage/price	Gini	Productivity	Profit rate
Mean	498,833,586	3.431	47.18778	0.726543	0.929227	0.442307
Standard deviation	760,320,082	0.320728	21.13353	0.073121	0.087259	0.107562
Min.	32,966,014.89	2.74	16.94451	0.560264	0.747229	0.165929
Max.	4,171,591,271	4.05	117.2105	0.866849	1.13264	0.679482

Table 14.4   Mortal agents, no interest, 47 runs to 2300 years ($n=47$)

Mortal	GDP	Unemployment	Wage/price	Gini	Productivity	Profit rate
Mean	19,709,930,254	9.687072	0.893945	0.446275	0.453629	0.704781
Standard deviation	33,146,598,710	6.451275	0.632817	0.04803	0.060956	0.172469
Min.	18,476	0.430323	0.081537	0.316765	0.306314	0.149154
Max.	159,347,000,000	37.61682	4.279715	0.542251	0.569656	0.913935

strongly correlated to productivity (population × productivity = real output). When population is fixed, productivity is the only causal factor left in this relationship. When population levels are allowed to change, real economic output is strongly influenced by population levels.

14.3   Eternal Population with Mutation

So far, the eternal population has been fixed and unchanging while the mortal population has been allowed to mutate and adapt. It is possible that it is the programming used for the mutation and adaption processes in the mortal population's program that is causing the divergence in the long-term trends.

Metaphoria is modified so that the eternal population is subjected to the same forces of starvation, old age, and mutation as the mortal population, except that there is no possibility of extinction. Whenever one agent dies, another is immediately born and inherits all the assets and qualities of the dead agent. When the new agent takes the dead agent's place, its propensities are put through the same mutation process applied to the mortal population. This puts the eternal agents through the identical program code as the mortal agents.

These experiments are like the Toy Trader model experiments in Sect. 10.2.1 where agent price algorithms are mutated but not subjected to a fitness test.

Another significant difference between the eternal and mortal populations are the possibility of changes in the population levels. If the resources and population are fixed as they are in the eternal population, the system can find more stability than when the ratio of resources to the population is constantly changing. Furthermore, where life is assumed, any imbalances of the monetary economy cannot impact the population level. This prevents the possibility of a feedback loop between the economy and the population on which it sits. Thus, a key layer of complexity is assumed away when an eternal population is used.

14.3.1   The Problem of Food Inheritance

Making the eternal population work with mutation required a modification of the inheritance process. In the mortal populations, inheritance works much as it does in the real world; parents tend to give to their children, children give back to their parents if the parents are still alive and the children have no children. If there are no living relatives, the inheritance goes to an agent close to the agent who died.

In the eternal population, the agent replacing the dead agent inherits everything. However, there is one key change between the two populations—the eternal population hands down all its harvested food, while in the mortal population, food is lost in inheritance.

If all harvested food is handed down from generation to generation, the food supply constantly increases (there is no food 'expiry date' in the simulation). In the case of the mortal population, a constantly increasing stock of food per capital, though the starvation rate does not change. In the eternal population, unrestrained food increase depresses starvation to more realistic levels. This is reflected by a more realistic life span (see Longevity).

Figure 14.5 shows the demographic charts for the eternal population with a constantly increasing food supply.

Charts

Real Production—Measures the actual productivity of the economy.

In the eternal population, if food is not inherited, the system unrealistically stratifies. The rich continue to live long lives while the poorer populations experience increasing mortality rates. An example of such a run is depicted in Fig. 14.6.

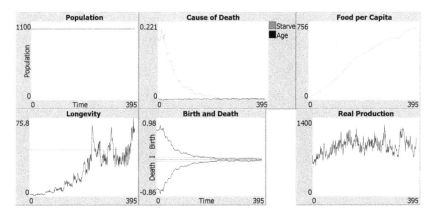

Fig. 14.5 Demographic charts, eternal population with mutation, food inherited, 1000 years

Note that the Longevity chart is near 0 while the two reference lines in the Birth and Death charts almost merge in the middle because of the chart compression caused by the high rates of birth and death. For this reason, allowing food to accumulate in the eternal population leads to a more realistic population. In contrast, Fig. 14.7 depicts the demographic charts for a simulation run with a mortal population and no food inheritance.

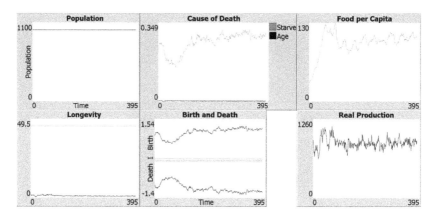

Fig. 14.6 Demographic charts, eternal population with mutation, no food inherited, 1000 years

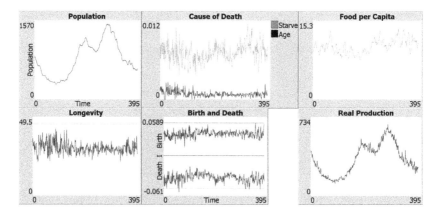

Fig. 14.7 Demographic charts, mortal population, no interest payments, no food inheritance, 1000 years

14.3.2   The Dynamics of Children

So far, none of the eternal populations has any children in their populations, whereas the mortal populations do. To get bring closer the programmed processes between the mortal population and the eternal population, children need to be introduced to the eternal population.

The mutation code in the mortal population works through reproduction. In the previous runs (Figs. 14.5 and 14.6) adults were reborn as unemployed adults with the same characteristics as their immediate ancestor except where mutation processes changed them (see Sect. 10.2.1). By doing so, the dynamics of children are included in the eternal mutated population.

Once children are introduced, food inheritance can be turned off and the simulation patterns are somewhat recognisable, even though longevity is suppressed. Figure 14.8 shows the demographic charts from simulation run using an eternal mutated population featuring children.

Other than including children in the population, there is no difference in the initiation or configuration of the simulation runs depicted in Fig. 14.6. The inclusion of children impacts the economic charts. Figure 14.9 shows the economic charts that accompany the demographic charts shown in Fig. 14.8.

Two of charts, Wage/Price Ratio and Profit Rate look relatively unchanged from eternal populations without children (Fig. 14.1). However, the Gini coefficient (of money) and the Per Capita Productivity looks markedly different.

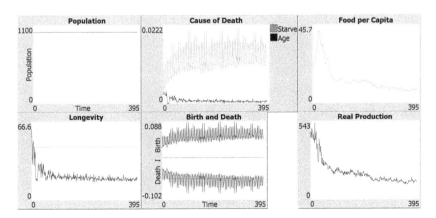

Fig. 14.8 Demographic charts, eternal population with mutation and children, no food inheritance

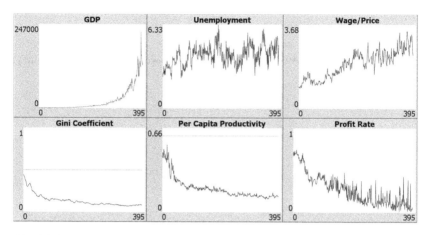

Fig. 14.9   Economic charts from the run depicted in Fig. 14.8

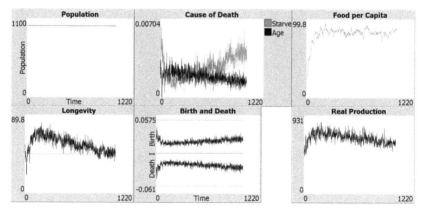

Fig. 14.10   Demographic charts, eternal population with fitness test, no interest

14.4   Eternal Population with a Fitness Test

This section explores the impact of a fitness test on the eternal population. The fitness test used in this section is much like the one used in the modified RobbyGA simulation (see Sect. 6.4). In the modified RobbyGA, only agents with low fitness scores died. In this simulation, agents with too little food die. As the ability to obtain food is highly correlated with available money, a money fitness test emerges.

Just as with RobbyGA, whenever an agent dies, the surviving agents give birth to a new agent, passing on its characteristics to the new agent. The reproduction and mutation processes are identical to those used in the mortal populations of Metaphoria except that the population level is fixed at 1000 by regulating reproduction. This means that individual agents are mortal, but the population is eternal. Notably, it is impossible for the population to go extinct, no matter what the economy does.

Figure 14.10 shows the demographic charts of an eternal population subjected to a money fitness test.

The first point of interest is how much healthier the population is overall (see longevity). Initially, the longevity matches the levels achieved by the hunter/gatherer economy (see Figs. 13.1 and 13.2). However, this did not occur as a result of market forces; otherwise, the other eternal populations would exhibit similarly high longevity rates. The only difference between this and other eternal populations is the inclusion of evolutionary prerequisites.

However, the dominant evolutionary fitness test has shifted from life to money. The effect of this can be seen in how life expectancy decreases over time (see longevity). Of interest is whether longevity is tied to the availability of food. If the per capita food supply declines before the longevity declined, then the cause is a systemic lack of food. With per capita food supply rising, the only cause left for starvation is maldistribution.

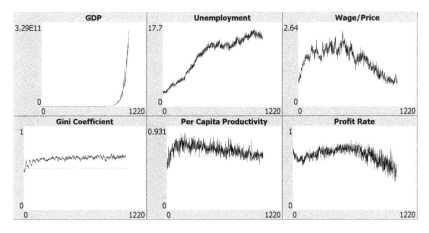

Fig. 14.11 Economic charts from the run depicted in Fig. 14.10

The charts show that not only can starvation increase in advance of a decline in the per capita food supply, the per capita food supply can go up while starvation figures are rising.

This is expected when there is a money fitness test combined with the tendency for money to distribute itself near to a 0.5 Gini coefficient.

The effect of the money fitness test is easier to see in the eternal populations than mortal populations, as the changing population levels of mortal populations impact the demographics and economic charts so that otherwise obvious trends can be overwhelmed by demographic changes.

The most notable change between eternal populations with and without a fitness test is that the introduction of a money fitness test brings the Profit Rates and Wage/Price Ratio to levels recognisable from mortal populations (Figs. 14.2 and 14.4). Figure 14.11 shows the economic charts for the eternal population featured in Fig. 14.10.

Overall, introducing a money fitness test to an eternal population moves the results noticeably closer to those of mortal population simulation runs with a similar fitness test. The trends, however, do not necessarily match. This is partly due to the fact that there are stochastic changes resulting from changing population levels—because of population changes, the random number generator has agents making different decisions between the two runs because the random number generator is accessed at different frequencies between the two runs.

A greater influence occurs when population is allowed to fluctuate. In this case, economic performance can impact population levels which in turn can impact economic performance. A model with eternal population levels prevent this layer of complexity from developing.

14.5   Summary

Economic models using eternal populations result in different long-term outcomes and trends than models with mortal populations. As the real world consists of mortal populations, these results question the utility of using standard equation-based economic models in the development of long-term theory and policy. The key reason is that eternal populations assume out a layer of complexity where the performance of the economy intersects with the well-being of population.

The models presented make no claim to successfully predicting the empirical long-term economic trends of a monetary economy. These results are presented with the understanding that the model used for this demonstration has not yet been completed. However, the influencing forces seem to be systemically broad rather than the result of model detail. One difference is the presence or absence of evolution. As was shown in Sect. 10.2.1, evolution seems to be the key force shaping economic patterns. Section 6.4 showed how evolution can arise simply by allowing poorer agents to starve to death while allowing successful agents to reproduce. Chapter 8 (the distribution of money) shows how inequality is likely to lead to starvation. Chapter 9 (system efficiency) demonstrates principles by which the market system is likely to be less efficient than earlier economic organisations. The results from the Metaphoria model match the results from the Toy Trader model in several areas.

Accordingly, those devising long-term economic theory and policy need to be aware that economic models using representative agents or eternal multi-agent populations are likely to lead to inaccurate long-term outcomes.

References

Epstein, J., & Axtell, R. (1996). *Growing artificial societies: Social sciences from the bottom up*. Washington, DC: MIT Press.

Hamill, L., & Gilbert, N. (2016). *Agent-based modelling in economics*. Hoboken, UK: Wiley.

Hartley, J. E. (2002). *The representative agent in macroeconomics*. London: Routledge.

CHAPTER 15

Summary and Final Comments

Abstract It is almost certain that the economy is a complex system. This research uses experiments to begin the process of building basic economic theory assuming the economy is a complex system. Most importantly, it examines how empirically present evolutionary prerequisites of markets and society go on to form evolutionary processes that can dominate price and distribution. While the linear-system economic theory taught in university courses around the world is useful for short-term analyses, it will likely fail in the long-term if the economy is a complex system. Knowledge of how trade behaves in a complex-system is crucial for any economist or policy-maker designing theory or policies for the long-term.

Keywords Complex-system · Linear-system · Evolution · Emergent behaviour · Price · Equality · Distribution · Efficiency · Population · Long-term · Short-term

If the economy is a scientifically complex system, then expanding economic investigations to include trade in a complex system is a necessary step. This is the first book exploring the basic behaviour of monetary trade in a complex system. Without this knowledge, it is very difficult to understand a market economy in general.

Experiments demonstrate that complexity directly impacts the distribution of money, system efficiency, and price determination in a market

© The Author(s) 2019 161
T. Gooding, *Economics for a Fairer Society*,
https://doi.org/10.1007/978-3-030-17020-2_15

system. Furthermore, the results offer a specific reason for persistent starvation in the presence of abundant food. A core economic function is the distribution of the goods created. Unless we agree that the lack of marketable productivity should be punishable by death, modern starvation is a failure of a core economic competency: distribution.

In the short run, not enough time passes for complex dynamics such as feedback, adaption, and emergent behaviour to form. In this case, the initial conditions dominate the outcome. This is where a linear-system economic analysis is most useful. However, as time passes, the initial conditions lose potency while more immediate factors, such as the last trading-price, become increasingly dominant. There is a point where long-term dynamics take over in determining the shape the system. At this point, a linear-system analysis may no longer apply.

As far as I am aware, this is the first research anywhere to experimentally explore the impact of evolution on price and distribution patterns. A key result of these experiments suggests that evolutionary prerequisites cause evolutionary forces to dominate the patterns in some markets, especially with regard to price. There is good evidence that supply and demand may not determine price in the long run in a complex system. This result has important implications as linear-system theory predicts that a market society's wealth is allocated by merit. This linear-system prediction rests on the assumption that price is determined by supply and demand in an efficient market. If this is not the case, if the rich and poor arise as a result of physical systemic forces rather than merit, then there are implications to policy if we want to build a fair society.

This work is built up slowly starting with an already established area of enquiry—the tendency for money to become exponentially distributed in a market system. Then it moves to explore the inverse relationship of computational effort with system efficiency and goes on to explore further elements that impact the efficiency of markets in a complex system. The combined results from these experiments help explain the experimental results involving price and the extreme inequality we see in the world.

The market economy is widely assumed to be the most efficient economic organisation ever devised by humankind. However, this assertion also rests on the basis that supply and demand determine price. The field of complexity suggests that different criteria are crucial for system efficiency. Complexity researchers have long known that increasing the computational load of the agents within a system, such as more consumer choice and more population, decreases market efficiency. Experiments in this book suggest that this is true for trade systems as well. It might be interesting to some that many of the equation-based economic models taught in economic classes rely on an assumption that consumers possess perfect knowledge, which is near to an infinite computational load. Not only is this least efficient configuration possible in a scientifically complex system, it also fails the laws of thermodynamics as infinite knowledge requires infinite power to process.

No one disputes a market economy's impressive throughput. The modern economy, using technology, utilises magnitudes more energy than any previous economy in the history of humankind. However, the combination of price inefficiency and the effects of an increasing computational load experienced by many agents suggests that high throughput may not be linked to high efficiency. Furthermore, evolutionary theory predicts that Adam Smith's 'invisible hand', as guided by price, will cause a relative drop in societal well-being, as the markets' evolutionary forces are aimed at wealth accumulation instead of the well-being of the population or life on the planet. This is supported by recently established ecological and societal trends.

Either the economy's main priority is the well-being of its population, which includes life on earth in general as that is what sustains us, or it is not. If it is, then the global market is an empirical failure, as we have an abundance of food and millions of people who are not getting enough, the threat of the global climate destabilising, serious degragation of the ecosystem, and potentially destabilising inequality. Certainly, there have been successes, but to look away from lethal problems because some people in the population experience success is not a recipe for social cohesion.

Our economic narrative is crucial to building a fair society. If a linear analysis of the economy leads us to believe that poor people do not contribute to society through their own inadequacies, we are in danger of creating a fundamentally unfair society if this is not the case. When the economic investigation is expanded to include a complexity analysis, there is good evidence that many people will necessarily be poor due to the intrinsic structure of market economies. In order to create a fair society, this needs to be recognised.

This work does not suggest that the rich are wrong or they should be attacked. Individually, rich are like everyone else; they are sometimes good and sometimes bad. Nor are impoverished people necessarily lazy, stupid, or unproductive members of society. The overall message of this research is that the terrible crises approaching global human society are not caused by poor decision-making (though no one is saying poor decisions were not made). Failures in distribution, extreme inequality, the collapsing ecosystem, and the changing climate are not necessarily mainly the result of human negligence, idiocy, or poor planning, but predictable results of the evolutionary prerequisites that have dominated modern society for centuries. We knew very little about the dynamics and capability of evolution prior to the complexity revolution that took place in the physical sciences in the 1970s. This is recent knowledge and there are still lags in the system. How much did you know about the impact of evolutionary prerequisites before you read this work?

What might be surprising for some people is that the economy, which is supposed to serve the people, is almost always modelled without people. This results in a natural tendency for policy-makers and voters to focus on the well-being of the economy rather than that of the people that the economy purports to serve. The narrative is simple: what is good for the economy is good for you. Or even more simply: 'It's the economy, stupid!' Perhaps that is why we live in a society where many feel they must bend themselves to serve the economy rather than the economy bending to serve them. If you think about it, this position suggests that the monetary economy is the result of natural laws while the human population (and life in general) is the artifice.

One step to changing this outcome is to build models where economy includes living populations. Some economist might object—people are for sociologists and psychologists, not economists. The argument is that economists deal with the amoral outcome of trade while others fight over the morality. This is beside the point. When the experimental question is asked: does the long-term outcome of an economic model change when a population of living agents is added—the answer is yes. Therefore, long-term economic modelling requires the inclusion of 'people' before we can suggest that we know the outcome of a monetary economy.

This is not to say that all economic models need to be agent-based models with mortal populations. As these experiments demonstrate, very simple models have a great deal to teach us. The simpler the model, the easier it is to focus on understanding how the system works in general. Sometimes, the specifics do not matter. For example, Keen (1995) showed that placing using accepted economic identities into a system dynamics model resulted in the reproduction of the 'great moderation' (Bernanke, 2004) and an event that greatly resembled the 2007 financial crash. Overall, these results suggest that those presenting a linear-system analyses, like Bernanke (Ibid), need to be careful in how they situate their results as the economy is most likely a complex system.

Overall, the value of this book rests on the extent to which the market economy is a complex system. If it is, then you now know the basic outcomes of trade and you are among the first to learn how to create repeatable evolutionary experiments in monetary economics, and their initial results.

Welcome to the leading edge.

REFERENCE

Keen, S. (1995). Finance and economic breakdown: Modeling Minsky's "financial instability hypothesis". *Journal of Post Keynesian Economics, 17*(4), 607–635.

Appendix:
Model Descriptions and Downloads

Toy Trader Model

See Fig. A1.

The full code can be seen and downloaded at https://www.comses. net/codebases/2fd53b66-31a8-4031-9ae6-d39d0b818d1b/releases/ 1.2.0/.

The downloaded model has the settings consistent with the money fitness test demonstrated in Fig. 10.8. To run the simulation in this configuration, press [Setup] and then press [Go].

The design concept for the Toy Trader model originated from a participative programming exercise in a PhD multi-agent programming workshop I delivered in the Pakistan Institute of Development Economics. The complex results made it evident that developing the simplest experimental trade model possible would be a useful exercise. A prose description of The Toy Trader model is available in Chapter 8.

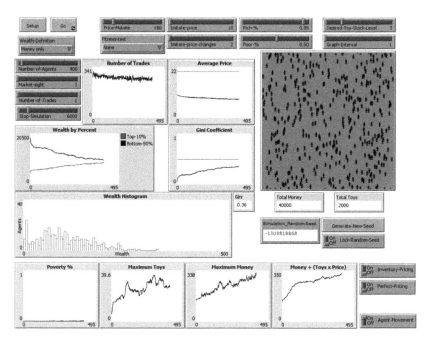

Fig. A1   Toy Trader interface

ODD

Overview

1. Purpose
Determine foundational emergent behaviour arising from trade.

2. Entities, state variables, and scales
The entities are traders who buy and sell goods. Traders seek to purchase a user set number of toys during each iteration at the lowest price.

3. Process overview and scheduling
On each iteration, all the traders move one patch in a random direction and attempt to purchase one toy at the lowest price they can find. The search distance can range from a radius of 1 patch to the entire environment, depending on the user setting Market-sight. If an agent sells a good, they adjust their selling price according to their inventory. The agent can be set to mutate price changes, imitate price, and/or imitate price changes.

Design Concepts

4. Design concepts
The basic principle is trade using price as the controller. If evolution is turned on, agents can imitate the price and pricing strategy of the most successful agents.

The rates of mutation and strategy adoption are determined by probabilities set by the user.

An agent seeking to purchase a toy searches according to a range set by the user. The agents only interact by purchasing and selling to one another.

Stochasticity changes depend on what features are activated. At the basic level, the order in which the agents take their turn is determined stochastically each iteration. If mutation or price imitation is turned on, the effects are determined by user set probabilities.

Observation frequency can be adjusted by the user, but usually each iteration is observed and include the system-wide average price, the sum of trades, and the Gini coefficient of the wealth designated by the user (money only, money + toys × average price, toys only). There is also a wealth histogram based on the wealth designation. There are four more charts used for reference only rather than reporting results. They include poverty and the maximum of the three wealth designations.

Details

5. Initialisation
The population is determined by the user and placed randomly in the environment. All agents start with 5 toys and 100 money. The price up variable is 1.0101 and the price down variable is 0.99.

6. Input data: none

7. Sub-models
In purchasing a toy, the buying agent seeks the lowest price within its detection range. If the buyer has enough money, the price is given to the seller and the seller gives one toy to the buyer. The seller then checks its inventory. If it is above 3, it will lower its selling price by $price_{new} = price_{old} \times$ its price down variable. If it is below 3, it will raise its selling price by $price_{new} = price_{old} \times$ its price up variable.

If mutation is turned on, the price-up and price-down variables will be randomly changed at a user-set probability. If imitate price is turned on, poor agents will set their price to that of rich agents at a user-set probability. If imitate price change is turned on, poor agents will set their price change variables (price-up and price-down) to that of rich agents at a user-set probability and then mutate that variable.

THREE-GOODS TRADER

See Fig. A2.

The full code can be viewed and downloaded at https://www.comses.net/codebases/5607355f-6078-465c-9fe0-3cbd44c3a1cd/releases/1.3.0/.

The downloaded model is set to a fitness test but [pricing-connection] is turned off so crayons and blackboards do not exhibit evolutionary patterns. To run the simulation in this configuration, press [Setup] and then press [Go].

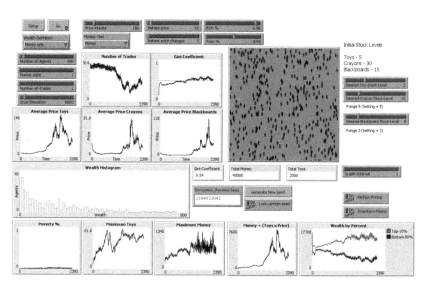

Fig. A2 Three-goods trader interface

For Chapter 11, the agents traded three goods instead of just one. The program changes were relatively simple. The code controlling the agents changed from:

repeat Number-of-Trades [trade-toys]
to,
repeat Number-of-Trades [trade-blackboards
trade-toys
trade-crayons]

Everything the agents did to trade Toys was duplicated with the new products, crayons and blackboards. However, the way prices changes were applied within the simulation changed.

In Fig. 11.2, the evolved price-up and price-down strategy was disconnected from the two new products. The prices of blackboards and crayons are raised and lowered in the following manner:

price up is: $price_{new} = price_{old} \times 1.0101$
Price down is: $price_{new} = price_{old} \times 0.99$

The code change from the standard pricing is trivial. For example, the standard code for altering the price of crayon is the following.

to change-price-up-c
  set price-c price-c * price-up
end

to change-price-down-c
  set price-c price-c * price-down
  if price-c < 0.5 [set price-c 0.5]
end

To alter this code, the following two changes (in bold) are made:

to change-price-up-c
  *set price-c price-c * **1.0101***
end

to change-price-down-c
  *set price-c price-c * **0.99***
  if price-c < 0.5 [set price-c 0.5]
end

DOUBLE AUCTION

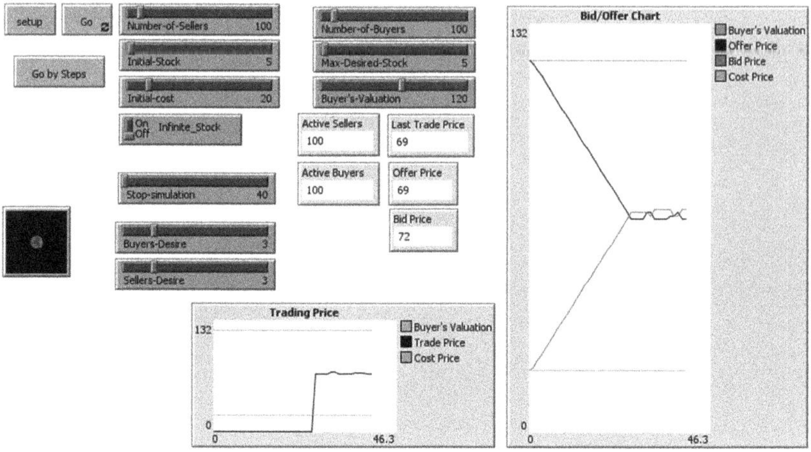

Fig. A3   Double auction interface

See Fig. A3.

The full code can be viewed and downloaded at https://www.comses. net/codebases/92f27d91-c0ed-44ef-93c4-d78c1c50499a/releases/1.1.0/.

To run the simulation in its current configuration, press [Setup] and then press [Go]. The [Go by Steps] button triggers a single iteration. The model is currently set up with sellers offering a finite number of goods and buyers possessing a satiating level. In this configuration, buyers and sellers will naturally stop trading as sellers run out of goods to sell and buyers are satiated. This happens at around 630 iterations.

This model replicates experiments in the literature.

Basically, there are buyers and sellers. The buyers' value and the sellers' cost are set by the user. The individual agents might vary from this value by up to 10%. Both buyers start bidding near the sellers' cost and the sellers start offering near the buyers' cost. They then adjust their bids in an attempt to create trade. Once trade occurs, the buyers and sellers continually try to improve their situation by trying to force their price in a direction favourable to themselves.

The Info tab in the simulation gives the full information about how to run this simulation.

METAPHORIA 2019

See Fig. A4.

The full code can be seen and downloaded at https://www.com-ses.net/codebases/191b6c6d-95f8-45ba-b33d-cab66988b628/releases/1.1.0/.

The model is currently at the same settings as Figs. 13.1 (hunter/gatherer) and 13.5 (monetary—with interest turned on). *Note* If you run the hunter/gatherer version at these settings, you will end up with a very high population and the simulation will run quite slowly. To hold the population down, reduce the resources by lowering the [max-renewable-resources] to around 15.

To run the simulation in its default configuration, press [Set H/G] and then press [Run H/G] to run the hunter/gatherer organisation. Press [Set Monetary] and then [Run Monetary] to run the simulation.

Metaphoria was designed to explore the basic forces of trade in more realistic conditions. As the impact of elements is understood, more will be added. This is the simplest trade model I could think to build using a mortal population.

Overview

1. Purpose

To test the basic forces arising from trade using a mortal population and compare its performance against a hunter/gatherer style of economy. It is also used to test the impact of a mortal population on economic prediction.

This model also can run in a hunter/gatherer mode. See Sub-models.

2. Entities, state variables, and scales

- The entities are banks, businesses, and agents. Agents carry money and food and possibly own a bank or a business and have children to feed. Agents are also employed or unemployed.
- Businesses carry employees, goods (food), and money. They may carry a loan.
- Banks carry money and loans.
- Patches carry food.

The simulation is linked to time through the reproduction which is assumed to be a maximum of 1 child per couple per year. The number of purchase cycles and pay periods are user-adjustable.

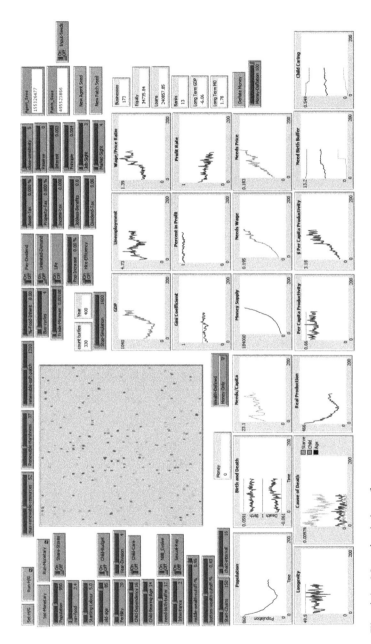

Fig. A4   Metaphoria interface

3. Process overview and scheduling

Businesses calculate their productivity from the amount of labour (from workers) available to work on their patch. The goods are placed in a store for selling. The worker pay is calculated based on productivity and the firms need for workers. Taxes are paid based on money in their account (asset tax) if that tax is turned on. Workers are hired or fired depending on workforce's requirements and profit status. Wages are adjusted according to workforce's requirements and profit status. If the money account is negative, a loan is sought. If there is no bank nearby, create a bank and assign ownership to a random agent. If profits exceed 2 × the wage bill, pay a dividend to the owner. Pay dividend tax if it is turned on. If there are no workers in the business, prepare to close business.

Workers add a year to their age and turned from a child into an adult at appropriate age (user-adjustable). If agents have money, taxes are applied if applicable (asset tax). If unemployed, seek a job. If there are no jobs available and the agent is on a productive patch with no business, start a business. Calculate how much food the agent requires and compare to stock of food. If food is required, buy food. If there is a propensity to set up a business, actively seek to set up a business. If unemployed and there is a propensity to explore, leave the area. If there is a propensity to seek new employment, quit their job and seek new employment. Reduce their stock of food by the required amount to remain alive. If their stock of food goes below 0, the agent dies and the eternal agent's assets are inherited according to user settings. If the probability of breeding is successful, a child is born.

If an agent is a child, seek food from their parent. If no food is available and the child has any money, seek to buy food. If food goes below 0, the agent dies.

Design Concepts

4. Design concepts

• Basic principles

The agents' behaviour are governed variables that were derived by stochastic processes. Successful agents survive and pass on their characteristics (sometimes mutated) to their offspring. Businesses derive their behaviour from their owner-agents. At the moment, there are no direct fitness tests being applied to businesses.

- Emergence
We are looking for how the monetary system interacts with a mortal population.

- Adaptation
Individual agents do not adapt throughout their lifetime, but the population adapts to changing conditions.

- Objectives
The objective of an agent is to stay alive and reproduce. As this is facilitated by wealth, an implicit objective is to be wealthy.

- Learning
There is no individual learning, though the population as a whole can learn through emergent processes.

- Prediction
There are no predictive measures in this simulation.

- Sensing
Agents can sense wages and prices within a radius set by the user. Agents can also sense patch productivity potential if starting a business. Businesses sense worker population, store inventory, money in their account, and profits each iteration.

- Interaction
Agents get work from businesses and buy food from businesses. Businesses hire, fire, and pay workers.

- Stochasticity
Stochastic processes are used extensively in the set-up. They are also used to mutate behaviour variables and in the implementation of propensities. They are also used in agent movement.

- Collectives
The only collectives are the workforces of businesses.

- Observation
A considerable part of the simulation programming is dedicated to generating information. Information is collected as needed and is frequently altered, depending on the needs of a particular investigation. For example, trades are counted and valued. Prices and wages are averaged and compared. System-wide aggregates such as money supply and productivity are graphed. Agents statistics and some behaviour variables are graphed.

Details

5. Initialisation

Almost all aspects of the simulation variables are user-adjustable. The population, the labour available per agent, and the required food per iteration are set by the user. All other aspects of behaviour and environment are user-set ranges that the program uses to stochastically determine the initial settings or can be adjusted while the simulation is running. The start and frequency of graphing are also user-adjustable.

6. Input data

No data are routinely inputted. It is possible to input random number generator seeds so that identical runs can be made, or identical starting points used.

7. Sub-models—The hunter/gatherer mode

The model is also capable of running in hunter/gatherer mode. The model uses identical processes to create the environments and agents, except the agents' behaviour only includes harvesting, reproducing, and moving.

The key difference is that there is no money in this version of the model. Agents seek to harvest patches. If more than one agent is on a patch, the harvest is evenly shared out. Agents move if they cannot harvest enough food to stay alive. There is a propensity to go off exploring the environment. If they fail, they will likely starve to death.

Metaphoria Modifications

Eternal Population Mutation

The full code can be seen and downloaded at https://www.comses.net/codebases/02cb5e0d-5a9d-4af0-b416-9bb5c2ed07e6/releases/1.0.0/.

Note that the [Set-Monetary] button has been renamed [Setup] to alert the user knows they are in a modified simulation. The downloaded model is set to Fig. 14.6 (no interest, no food inherited).

This modification was simple. In the original simulation, eternal agents did not die or reproduce. As the mutation code operates at birth, the agents needed to be allowed to die. When an eternal agent 'dies', its behaviour variables were run through the same mutation code as is used by the mortal population, its age variable was changed to 0, and it was made unemployed. This way the population level never changed.

In Netlogo, 'breed' gives agents unique behaviour. In Metaphoria, an 'adult' can get a job while a 'child' cannot. In the mutation version of Metaphoria, there is a switch called [eternal-children] that will change the breed of a newly born agent from 'adult' to 'child'. This gives the agent the behaviour of a child until the agent reaches the age of maturity. Before this modification, all eternal agents lived and died as adults.

Eternal Population Fitness Test

The full code can be seen and downloaded at https://www.comses.net/codebases/72f3d64a-eebd-458f-af98-a16929ce7799/releases/1.0.0/.

Note that the [Set-Monetary] button has been renamed [Setup] to alert the user knows they are in a modified simulation. The downloaded model is set to Fig. 14.10 (no interest).

Another simple modification. Instead of the behaviour of the dying agent being mutated and recycled to 'new' agent, the characteristics of a surviving living agent are given to the new 'agent', along with whatever money and businesses the dying agent might have had. This is the same mechanism used in the RobbyGA- modified simulation.

Except for inheritance and self-determination in terms of reproduce, all programmed processes used in the mortal population were used in this population.

RobbyGA with starvation

See Fig. A5.

The full altered code used in this work can be seen and downloaded at https://www.comses.net/codebases/e7c7c784-41c9-47a0-91b7-eb5426a9d8cd/releases/1.3.0/.

The downloaded model has the same settings as the end of Fig. 6.4.

This is the modification made to the RobbyGA model to make it more like reality and to allow for the user to adjust the evolutionary strength.

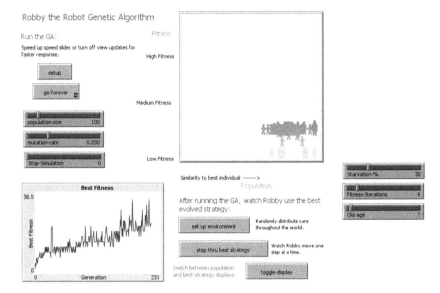

Fig. A5   RobbyGA with starvation

INDEX

181

CPSIA information can be obtained
at www.ICGtesting.com
Printed in the USA
LVHW071559290419
615921LV00009B/275/P